MW00366816

Seeking Life

Esther de Waal is one of today's most popular authors writing in the field of spirituality. She lives in Herefordshire, close to the border between England and Wales, having returned to the countryside where she grew up. She spends two months each winter in Washington DC as the Senior Fellow of the Cathedral College, where her teaching centres on the development of the religious imagination. A sense of place has always been important, and it was the buildings and the landscape that originally encouraged her to explore the Benedictine, Cistercian and Celtic traditions. Although her main interests are her garden and her increasing number of grandchildren, she also finds time to write, to take retreats and to travel – feeling a particular connection with Southern Africa.

Other titles by Esther de Waal, available from Liturgical Press

A Life-Giving Way: A Commentary on the Rule of St. Benedict

Esther de Waal comes to the Rule of St. Benedict as a lay woman who has studied the Rule and striven to live it. Benedict has been for her both supportive and challenging, both guide and prophet. His Rule asks not for blind obedience and conformity but for personal responsibility. While the Rule offers much to those seeking a pattern to the structure of their day-to-day, "exterior" life, which de Waal's previous commentaries have addressed, this commentary focuses on what Benedict tells us about the interior life. It takes the shape of prayerful reflections on his words of wisdom regarding the disposition of the heart. It leads the reader, as the Rule was meant to lead the novice, to answer the very personal question we must all, as Christians, answer: "Am I truly seeking God?" Includes a copy of the Rule.

978-0-8146-2358-9

Lost in Wonder: Rediscovering the Spiritual Art of Attentiveness

In *Lost in Wonder*, Esther de Waal uses the everyday circumstances of our lives—the restrictions and frustrations as well as the gifts and opportunities—as our own way to God. By teaching us how to be attentive to all the seemingly small and insignificant things, she shows how they become windows through which the light of Christ can shine to dispel darkness, illuminate our understanding, and speak to our deepest needs. As we recover the gift of childlike wonder we begin to see that spiritual fruitfulness does not depend on our anxious performance, but is a gift we may receive freely.

978-0-8146-2992-5

Seeking God: The Way of St. Benedict, Second Edition

For over fifteen hundred years St. Benedict's Rule has been a source of guidance, support, inspiration, challenge, comfort and discomfort for men and women. It has helped both those living under monastic vows and those living outside the cloister in all the mess and muddle of ordinary, busy lives in the world. Esther de Waal's *Seeking God* serves as an introduction to this life-giving way and encourages people to discover for themselves the gift that St. Benedict can bring to individuals, to the Church, and to the world, now and in the years to come.

978-0-8146-1388-7

Seeking Life

The Baptismal Invitation of the
Rule of St. Benedict

Esther de Waal

LITURGICAL PRESS
Collegeville, Minnesota

www.litpress.org

First published in 2009 by the Canterbury Press Norwich
(a publishing imprint of Hymns Ancient & Modern Limited,
a registered charity)
13–17 Long Lane, London EC1A 9PN, UK

www.scm-canterburypress.co.uk

Published in the United States of America by
Liturgical Press, Collegeville, Minnesota 56321

Library of Congress
Cataloging-in-Publication data available

ISBN 978-0-8146-1880-6

For Zoe

Zoe with her mother at Eardisley font

Contents

Preface and Acknowledgements

I owe thanks to many places and many people in the writing of this book. Both sides of the Atlantic have played their part. Canon Jim Fenhagan and Canon Howard Anderson, the Wardens of the College of Preachers, subsequently the Cathedral College in Washington DC, welcomed me into the life of the College community for two months each year, which brought me hospitality, friendship and conversation in a warm and stimulating environment. This book could never have been written without the Woodstock Center at Georgetown University, in which I found a library of incomparable resource, with the material unavailable in the depths of the Welsh border countryside where I live. Its access to open shelves allowed me to wander and explore widely, and find material not only for this book but also for the series of lecture courses I have been giving at the same time. My warmest thanks go to Fr Leon Hooper SJ and his colleagues.

The practical help that was urgently needed to allow me to finish this book in the spring of 2008 came from the patient teaching of Zoe Maslin of Rowlestone Mill and the incomparable expertise of Ray Rose who dealt with my technological dramas with understanding and enjoyment.

Throughout this undertaking I have been supported in prayer by the sisters of the community at Tymawr, the Society of the Sacred Cross, the Anglican community with whom I have been so closely associated over many years. They are a few miles away, across the border in Wales. My own cathedral, of Hereford, has fulfilled its role as a mother church, bringing an excellence of liturgy, music and preaching – a source of beauty and energy for which I am deeply grateful. My debt to the yearly experience of the Easter Vigil, which has played such a seminal role in the genesis of this book, however, crosses the boundaries of the Anglican and Roman Catholic Churches and I must mention the names together of the Dean, the Very Revd Michael Tavinor, and of Fr Michael Evans OSB, parish priest of St Francis Xavier, Hereford, and Benedictine monk of Belmont Abbey.

My thanks therefore cross the divides of England and Wales, America and Britain, Anglican and Catholic – which is just as it should be for someone who lives in a borderland, for my greatest support has been my own home, the garden, the stream and water-fall, the orchard of this cottage which was given by my father to my husband and our four small boys forty years ago this spring. As I kept the anniversary on 21 March (this being the traditional date for the exchange of property in the country) I reflected with gratitude what it has brought me: the stability which has earthed me in times of much travelling, and a gentle rhythm of changing times and seasons, which has become a very essential undercurrent of my life.

My deepest debt is of course to St Benedict and the Rule which has continued to play such a vital role in my life over the years since my first encounter with the Benedictine tradition at Canterbury. My life has changed since then but the Rule remains a source of continuing support and challenge. Written for a community, it made sense in the years of my family life, but it has also allowed me to come to terms with life on my own in the past ten years. The vows bring me the strength to change and build as each new chapter of my life unfolds, and I know that this will continue until the day of my death.

This is a very personal book, and the way in which I handle my subject and the interpretation that I bring must be seen as entirely my own, and my responsibility. My hope is that my readers will be able to identify with my approach and that they will find here something of the excitement that I found in the writing of it.

ESTHER DE WAAL

Feast of St Benedict, 11 July 2008

List of Illustrations

I

BAPTISM

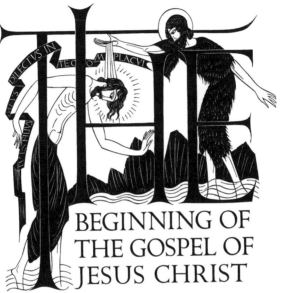

BEGINNING OF
THE GOSPEL OF
JESUS CHRIST

In those days Jesus came from Nazareth of Galilee and was baptized by John in the Jordan. And just as he was coming up out of the water, he saw the heavens torn apart and the Spirit descending like a dove on him. And a voice came from heaven, "You are my Son, the Beloved; with you I am well pleased."

Introduction

This book was originally written to meet an earlier deadline, which, however, never materialized because my antiquated, indeed antediluvian and archaic, word-processor met its death the previous week, and as a result everything went either into limbo or, some sections (notably the references and quotations), into undecipherable hieroglyphics. I could do nothing about it for some time because in the following months I was, as always in the winter, in Washington DC at the Cathedral College. A heavy teaching programme left little time for writing or research and when I returned to England just before Palm Sunday I immediately found myself plunged into Holy Week and Easter.

The reading I had been doing in preparation for writing the book meant that I entered, as I had never done before, into the liturgical life of the Triduum, those days from Good Friday to Easter. It became a powerful three-day experience, and I tried to keep it, in spite of many other demands, as it should be kept – as 'a time of vigilant prayer in preparation for the passing over from the old to the new'.[1] This meant that the Easter Vigil itself, and above all the renewal of baptismal promises, gained a depth and meaning that they had never had before.

As a result I then began to rewrite the book in a totally different way, and I was grateful that an apparent catastrophe should become the occasion of a new start. The change was that I decided to make Easter (or more strictly the Easter Vigil in the context of the Triduum) my starting point. My central theme still remained the renewal of the baptismal covenant, and although it takes place in particularly splendid and significant circumstances during the Easter Vigil, I would not want this book to be seen only in that context. Of course if it is read during Lent that would be extremely appropriate, but I hope that it will not be seen only in the context of Lenten reading.

When the idea of vocation is so often used in a specialized and limited way to apply to those responding to the call to enter the religious life, the ordained ministry or some special office in the Church, it is good to remind ourselves that baptism remains the essential foundation on which all Christian life is built.[2]

Baptism is the vocation that we all share as Christians. This book is written for all of us who have been baptized and for whom our baptismal promises are a lifelong commitment. Yet, although we have the chance to renew the covenant of baptism time and again throughout our lives, I do not find a great deal of attention being paid to the preparation for that renewal. But for those of us baptized as infants, when we come to think about baptism in adulthood many of us may find that we can now enter into that experience much more fully and are able to appreciate its riches. Above all it presents us with a world of imagery and symbolism that fuels the imagination. It brings us a feast of glorious teaching from the early Fathers which feeds the mind. It is liturgy at its most magnificent with language that rejoices the heart. It can become a source of strength for our continuing Christian discipleship, and remind us of the many others whom we join to form the body of Christ and for whom this has been the crossing of a threshold opening up into a new and fuller life.

Baptism is given once (frequently in infancy), but we also have
the chance to renew it time and again throughout our lives.
Although it is increasingly popular for this to be at the Easter Vigil
there are many other opportunities as well. I can think of three very
different times in my own life, in circumstances which cross
boundaries of place and denomination. In May 1982 I was present
in Canterbury Cathedral on the historic occasion of the visit of
Pope John Paul. In his address he spoke of how we were about to
renew our baptismal vows together: 'Anglicans and Catholics and
other Christians, as a clear testimony to the one sacrament of
baptism by which we have been joined in Christ . . . In this way the
renewal of our baptismal vows will become a pledge to do all in our
power to co-operate with the grace of the Holy Spirit, who alone
can lead us to the day when we will profess the fullness of our life
together.' And then, standing in front of the chair of St Augustine
before the high altar, flanked on one side by the Moderator of the
Free Churches and on the other by the Archbishop of Canterbury,
that vast congregation, filling the nave to capacity and with crowds
of people standing outside, all together joined in renewing their
baptismal promises. To the ringing declaration of the Pope, 'This is
the faith of the Church,' we gave the resounding response, 'This is
our faith.'

Several years later I found myself in the National Cathedral in
Washington DC for the feast of the Epiphany, where the then
Presiding Bishop of the Episcopal Church, Frank Griswold, was
the celebrant and again we renewed our baptismal promises. The
Epiphany is another of the festivals of the Church when Jesus'
baptism in the Jordan is recalled, and as a result brings another
opportunity for us to recall the significance of our own baptism.
The Magi and the Jordan are juxtaposed in a sermon for Epiphany
by St Peter Chrysologus:

Today the wise man ponders in profound amazement what he
sees there . . .
Today Christ entered the riverbed of the Jordan . . .

Today the Holy Spirit floats over the waters in the form of a dove, so that by this sign it might be known that the world's universal shipwreck has ceased.[3]

But every year I am always at home for Holy Week and Easter, so I have the certainty of knowing that I shall be keeping the Easter Vigil in the mother church of my own diocese. Hereford Cathedral is very close to the Roman Catholic church of St Francis Xavier, where the parish priest is a monk from the nearby Benedictine community of Belmont Abbey. On alternate years the vigil starts in one or other church and then, after a procession down the main street of the city, concludes in the other. Thus I know that at a particular point in the service – after the long readings, and the lighting of the new fire, and the Exsultet – I shall find myself standing and facing the font, recalling my baptismal covenant. Whether that font is made of solid Norman stone or is an ornately gilded nineteenth-century design, the questions will remain the same, spoken either by an Anglican cathedral dean or a Roman Catholic Benedictine monk. I make my response, mingling my voice with those of the large congregation which surrounds me, made up equally of Anglicans and Roman Catholics, and as I do so I recall the words of Pope Leo the Great:

> In the unity of our faith and baptism
> We enjoy an undivided fellowship
> And dignity common to us all.[4]

Yet do I really prepare myself sufficiently for this moment? Is it too easy to take it for granted? Would it mean more if I took time beforehand in preparation, through reading and prayer? These are the questions that underlay my wish to write this book – in the first instance for myself, but then increasingly I wanted to share it with others. I felt that something important and splendid had been lost to us, had somehow slipped from our grasp and I wanted to recover it.

I found that my exploratory study of baptism in the early centuries of the Church took me into the areas not only of theology, history and liturgy, but also of anthropology, architecture and ritual. I found that the teaching given in preparation for baptism made thoroughly exciting reading, full of dramatic language, energizing and stirring of the feelings because it was so imbued with a sense of the urgency of turning towards this promise of life and freedom. It made as much use of the visual as the verbal, and all the five senses were involved. I discovered the importance of image, symbol and storytelling in the rite itself. I realized that the phrase *baptismal covenant* is misleading if it seems only to carry cerebral or legalistic connotations, but that as soon as it is seen in the context of the Old Testament covenant it becomes something quite different. The covenant of the Old Testament is something glorious, demanding all our heart and mind, and carries a sense of warmth. The further I read, the more I realized how baptism involved the whole of the self – so that people were brought face to face with nothing less than their full humanity.

Whenever we enter a church we are reminded that baptism is the foundation of the Christian life, its starting point. The font is there to greet us, in all the many forms that it may take. Where I live I am surrounded by churches with huge, deep Norman fonts, standing fonts in which the child could be totally immersed – since the practice of adult baptism had largely fallen into disuse by the tenth century. Later on, fonts might become more elaborate, ornate, even ornamental. But whatever the shape they are there in order that, in the words of the seventeenth-century poet and parish priest George Herbert, people may 'call to mind their baptism often'.

Rivers, flowing water, pools were used in the earliest days, and it was not until the fourth or fifth century that baptisteries began to appear. At first these were square or rectangular, making connection with the cubic mausoleum which was common at this time, so that the image of the font is that of a sepulchre. But, from the fifth century, other images also begin to creep in. We find the circular font – the feminine shape, a reminder of the womb – while the octagon brings a reminder of the seven days of creation and the eighth day, the day of resurrection. So here we find the visual expression of the two integral elements of baptism: birth and rebirth, death and resurrection. This symbolic expression of a circular font is continued in many more recent fonts and baptisteries, one of the most dramatic and effective examples being at St John's Abbey in Collegeville, Minnesota, where the first thing to greet anyone as they come through the great north doors of the magnificent abbey church are the steps leading down to a pool, set low in the floor, with the movement of circulating water.

What first drew me to this interest was discovering the connection between the Prologue of the Rule of St Benedict and early teaching on baptism. Scholars have long recognized that the Prologue is a fragment of a baptismal catechesis, based on a homily given for those about to be baptized. But this has tended to remain a nugget of information tucked away in academic commentaries, or in a passing reference in a footnote, and therefore not widely known. Yet once the connection has been made it brings another dimension to the reading of the Prologue. St Benedict not only includes material found in baptismal catechesis, such as the psalm commentary commonly used in addressing candidates for baptism, but all the underlying imagery which brings such a dramatic element to baptism: death and life, light and darkness, the battle, the journey and, above all, the figure of the risen Christ.

The result of this has been that I have found myself once again drawn back to the text of the Rule – more specifically, the text of the Prologue. I have once again turned to Benedict as the teacher whose concern is to lead his disciples into the way of fullness of life. Rereading the Prologue in the context of baptism, after I had read much other early material (some of it included in the anthology at the conclusion of this book), brought fresh depth to familiar words, nuances and resonances which I now became aware of because I was seeing them in this new context.

I have therefore drawn out of the Prologue certain themes that relate to baptism and I hope that by presenting them in this way this book may serve the purpose of helping us to reflect on our baptismal vocation. I hope that it can be seen as *lectio*, that reflective reading, mulling over words and turning them into prayer, which is a particular monastic art. In the introduction to his translation of the Rule intended for lay people, Fr Patrick Barry makes this point very clearly:

> The Prologue of the Rule is itself inspired by the spirit of *lectio* . . . it penetrates to the deepest meanings of our Christian life . . . timeless call to inner personal change, growth, development through the Word of God.[5]

This return to Benedict seems particularly appropriate since the later date of its publication means that this book will appear almost twenty-five years to the day since the publication of my *Seeking God: The way of St Benedict*. The tradition of monastic spirituality and, above all, the Rule has played an immensely significant part in my life over these past years. I constantly return to the Rule itself, to a text that is at once familiar and yet always new. It has been at the root of my belief and practice, and it has brought me simultaneously support and encouragement while at the same time presenting me with the prospect of a lifelong journey of continuing and never-ending transformation. That glorious assertion with which Benedict ends the Prologue, that its goal is that by faithfully following the way 'we shall through patience share in the sufferings of Christ that we may deserve also to share in his kingdom. Amen.'

The accidental book

This seems a good moment in which to tell the story of how *Seeking God* came to be written only as the result of a series of accidents. In the 1980s Collins, still operating under the shadow of Lady Collins and long before the appearance of Rupert Murdoch, was the only publishing house to produce a Lent book – the Archbishop of Canterbury's Lent book – which was always commissioned well in advance, generally written by a pillar of the ecclesiastical establishment and, of course, until then only by a man. When there was a crisis with the manuscript due for 1984, the editor Sarah Baird-Smith approached me and asked if I would expand on a piece that I had recently written for the community at West Malling in Kent, on the subject of the Rule of St Benedict and family life. Even this had been written by chance, for the nuns had originally asked my husband and myself to do it together, but when he was ill I had to take over, which resulted in writing for the first time in my life on a religious topic.

In 1983 therefore I was given six months to produce a book-length manuscript on the theme of the Rule in the life of the lay Christian. This was something of a challenge since those were the years in which I had four young sons, was teaching for the Open University, and there were all the many demands that fell to my lot as the wife of the Dean of Canterbury. At that time I had visited only two Benedictine communities – the Anglican nuns in Kent, and the Roman Catholic monks and sisters of Bec-Hellouin (whose friendship with Canterbury dated back to the years of Lanfranc and St Anselm and was strengthening during these years through frequent visits and exchanges). If I had known more of the life and practice of current Benedictine monasticism, I probably would never have had the temerity to have embarked on the writing of the book. I wrote it with lay people like myself in mind, never having any idea of it being seen by professed religious. However, not only did Benedictine communities read it, both in Britain and in America, but they then encouraged their oblates and associates and visitors to read it, and as a result it has been translated into many languages worldwide. Surely this can only be seen as 'God's celestial time-keeping' – the inimitable words of Canon Dick Milford who in old age (after a career that included the founding of Oxfam) used to come and visit us and talk about God's sense of humour – to which I would add, with gratitude, the grace of the time and the place that put me in a situation that was to change my life in such a totally unexpected way.

Preparing for Easter

Holy Saturday

Good Friday is familiar. Easter is one of the great festivals, celebrated by the secular world as well as being for Christians the pivot of their year. But Holy Saturday seems to be the forgotten day of the Christian calendar. Most of us are far too busy – making preparations for the Easter celebrations, cooking, decorating the church, travelling, organizing family holidays. So how, unless we have the good fortune to be able to go away on retreat, do we handle this day, make it a time of emptiness, of waiting, seeing it as the empty space, which is yet full, coming between two powerful liturgies? In her poem 'Holy Saturday', the American poet Bonnie Thurston reminds us that it is the seventh day, the day on which God rested 'from making, from being un-made':

Christ has died.
Life is hidden
In God's obscurity

I love this day
of silent waiting
when fasting is over,
feasting not begun,
when pain is past
but flesh not quickened
This is where we live,
this human space,
waiting before the cave
in the tarnished garden
where it all began
and ended
to begin anew,
we hope, forever.[6]

Few days are more mysterious.

What is happening?
Today there is a great silence over the earth,
a great silence, and stillness,
a great silence because the King sleeps . . . [7]

These are the opening words from an ancient homily for Holy
Saturday by an unknown author who shows us the scene set in all its
drama:

He wishes to visit those who sit in darkness and in the shadow of
death. He goes to free the prisoner Adam and his fellow-prisoner
Eve from their pains, he who is God, and Adam's son.
    The Lord goes in to them holding his victorious weapon, his
cross . . . And grasping his hand he raises him up, saying: 'Awake,

O sleeper, and arise from the dead, and Christ shall give you light.'

Orthodox theologians have always said – surely rightly – that the actual moment of the resurrection cannot be depicted (any more than the moment of the creation or the incarnation). The classical Easter icons choose to show the effect of God's saving action, the moment of liberation, breaking down the doors of the underworld. How can we even begin to imagine it? The crucified, with his bleeding body, his wounds still raw, descends into the depths of darkness. Christ stands on a narrow bridge (is it the cross?), spanning a dark pit, and he is grasping Adam by one hand and Eve by the other. He is in a robe of glory, with a halo, and he is about to bring them up out of that darkness into the realm of light. This is Christ who has allowed himself to be overcome by death so that 'death would gulp him down into the innermost depths of the world', as Karl Rahner puts it.[8] Is this something even beyond personal salvation? Is it the earth itself that is now transfigured, 'an earth that is set free, that is untwisted . . . that is forever redeemed from death and from futility'?[9] These must remain questions to which we cannot know the answer, and it seems to me that that is right.

For Holy Saturday is above all a day of silence. There is a hidden intensity to this day and it is once again the artists who have tried to capture it for us in visual terms. The descent of Christ into the underworld lends itself to magnificent depiction, above all in the work of the iconographers. He is shown not as captive but as conqueror, the deliverer of those imprisoned, the bringer of light to the furthest depths of human experience. Although the Gospels tell us nothing of this mysterious event, Peter speaks of it on the day of Pentecost (Acts 2.14–39) and, in the third chapter of his first epistle, 'he went and preached unto the spirits in prison' (1 Peter 3.19). It clearly was widely known in medieval Europe, since – something which never ceases to surprise and delight me – it has been chosen in the mid-twelfth century to be represented on the font at Eardisley a small church in the remote border country between England and

Wales. It is a dramatic and dynamic scene, portrayed with extra-ordinary vigour and richness. Christ is dragging Adam out of a limbo of twisted knots, rather like clinging tentacles. (An antiquarian brochure, written by someone who had no idea of the context, described it as a man being pulled out of a thorny hedge, and somehow I always felt that this homely interpretation was no bad way of catching something of the difficulty and discomfort of how entangled we become and how we need the help of a strong hand to drag us upward.) Christ is clutching Adam firmly by the wrist, with a strength and determination of grasp that is virtually tangible. On Christ's left shoulder a dove is perched, and in his right hand he is carrying a cross, which resembles a staff. His figure is leaning forward, almost bent, as he moves with such urgency. And then we also have here the magisterial figure of God the Father, seen holding a book so that the scene becomes trinitarian. Did the sculptors, or their patron, recognize how appropriate this was for a font? We have no way of knowing. But for any of us seeing it today it gives us a portrayal of the saving grace of the Godhead, just as for generations of families bringing children to be christened here it must have spoken in its own terms in ways that we cannot begin to imagine.[10]

The significance of the scene, however it may be portrayed, in whatever medium and at whatever date, is not, as Rowan Williams is keen to point out, about rescuing those who are in 'hell' in the sense that they are for ever cut off from God. But they are imprisoned, unfulfilled, their growth towards God halted. We might say that they were languishing in their 'frozenness', but when Christ's hand touches them something new becomes possible. Moving into the heart of human longing and incompletion, Christ overcomes the locked gates of death, the frozen lives cut short, in the act of the new creation that we are witnessing.[11]

This anonymous writer continues, telling us how Christ addresses Adam and his fellow-prisoners with the promise of new life:

Awake, O sleeper,
and arise from the dead,

and Christ shall give you light.
Come forth . . . Have light . . . Rise . . .
I command you: Awake, sleeper.
I have not made you to be held prisoner in the underworld.
Arise from the dead; I am the life of the dead.
Arise, O man, work of my hands,
arise, you who were fashioned in my image.
Rise, let us go hence . . .

Easter

Easter is the pivotal moment of the Christian year. It is prefaced by forty days of preparation and followed by fifty days of rejoicing. Benedict tells us to 'look forward to holy Easter with joy and spiritual longing'. He himself had a memorable experience of Easter when he was in the cave at Subiaco, that time of silence and solitude, spent, in the memorable words of St Gregory, 'holding himself still before the gaze of God'. He is so deep in prayer that he is totally unaware that it is Easter. But God alerts a local priest to find the cave and to bring him Easter greetings – to which Benedict looking up from his prayers responds, 'Easter indeed it is brother because you are here.' In this man, the first human being that he has encountered for many months, he sees the first fruits of the resurrection, the risen Christ. The gaze that he now turns on the other penetrates through the externals to the true self, the risen self in Christ. (Later on when he comes to write the Rule he will include what has become one of his most well-known aphorisms: 'Let everyone who comes be received as Christ,' and it is tempting to think that he had this formative moment in mind so that, once again, we find him writing out of his own experience.)

The Easter festival has inspired magnificent prose and poetry, sophisticated works of art and humble verse. It is the time to shout Alleluia – as this traditional song does so joyously!

The whole bright world rejoices now,
Hilariter, hilariter!
The birds do sing on every bough,
Alleluya, alleluya!

Then shout beneath the racing skies,
Hilariter, hilariter!
To him who rose that we might rise,
Alleluya, alleluya![12]

This is hardly surprising, for Easter deals with what is timeless: the movement from dark and light, from dying and death, to resurrection and new life. For Benedict also tells us, 'Keep death daily before your eyes.' Here is paradox, tension. To think about Easter, and of course baptism in the context of Easter, faces us with paradox and with mystery, above all the paschal mystery.

For at the heart of Easter we come face to face with the figure of the risen Christ:

I am the Christ.
It is I who destroyed death,
who triumphed over the enemy,
who trampled Hades underfoot,
who bound the strong one
and snatched man away to the heights of heaven;
I am the Christ.

Then in words put into his mouth in this homily, the paschal Christ addresses each one of us:

It is I who am your forgiveness,
the lamb slain for you;
it is I who am your ransom, your life,
your resurrection, your light,
your salvation, your king.
I am bringing you to the heights of heaven.[13]

But it is not only what is written or depicted about Easter – it is the experience itself, both individually and corporately, which tells us so much. One of the most moving examples of what this can mean comes from the account of the Irish pilgrims who went to spend Easter in Rome in 631, coming 'as children to their mother'. They found themselves staying in one of the pilgrim hostels that clustered under the walls of the great basilica: 'And they were in one lodging in the church of St Peter with a Greek, a Hebrew, a Scythian, and an Egyptian at the same time at Easter.' Being there together at Easter with people from other nations gave them the shared experience of the universality of the Church. It had such a profound effect that on their return home they convinced their fellow Christians of southern Ireland to change the date of Easter to coincide with that of Rome – some thirty years before the rest of the Celtic Church.[14]

The celebration of Easter not only made Christian believers aware of the unity of the Church in other times and places, it also made them aware of their connectedness to the natural world itself, the ebb and flow of creation. In the *Letter to Nechtan*, Bede speaks of the whole universe being involved:

> We are commanded to keep the full moon of the paschal month after the vernal equinox, the object being that the sun should first make the day longer than the night and then the moon can show to the world her full orb of light because the 'Sun of righteousness with healing in his wings' (Matt. 4.2), that is, the Lord Jesus, overcame all the darkness of death by the triumph of his resurrection.[15]

Bede goes into greater deal on the connection of Easter with the created world when he writes of how the timing of the Pasch is central to both creation and redemption:

> when the equinox is passed, that the shadow of death may be vanquished by the true light. At the turn of the moon, to show

how the Glory of the mind is turned from earthly things to heavenly ones on the Lord's Day, when the light shows the triumph of
Christ and our own Resurrection.[16]

Elements from many traditions and sources inevitably flow into
this one great, central feast. In pre-Christian times the people of
northern Europe would gather together on a hilltop to light enormous bonfires to their gods now that winter was past and spring
was coming, gathering around the flames as they pleaded for the
return of new life. We picture that famous scene of the Christian era
when St Patrick on the hill of Slane, in full view of the Irish high
king on the hill of Tara, lit the first fire of Easter, causing such alarm
to the watching courtiers who predicted that this was a fire that
once lit would never be extinguished.

In the northern hemisphere where Easter fits in with the emer-
gence of new life after the cold and the sleep of winter, it is quite
naturally a part of rural consciousness, and as a result lends itself to
some charming local traditions which we occasionally get the
chance to glimpse. Francis Kilvert, the Victorian country priest and
diarist, tells what went on in his neighbourhood (which is also my
own countryside of the Welsh border country). He describes how it
was the custom on Easter Sunday morning for the villagers to go to
a nearby pool 'to see the sun dance and play in the water, and
the angels who were at the Resurrection playing backwards and
forwards before the sun'. They were not there for any particular
purpose, they had no message, no gift of healing, they were there
simply to go to and fro over the water. While it was something
shared it was at the same time intensely private and individual, as a
contemporary Welsh poet, Ruth Bidgood, recognizes when she tells
us in her poem 'Resurrection Angels' how solid-seeming villagers
stared enchanted watching the sun dance and play, as

In dazzle they half-saw
great shining shapes, swoop frolicking
to and fro, to and fro.

This much was shared
expected; day and place had their
appropriateness, their certainties.
The people had no words to tell
the astonishment, the individual bounty –
for each his own dance in the veins,
brush of wings over the soul.[17]

The Easter Vigil

It is hardly surprising then that the liturgy of the Triduum, the three days of Good Friday, Holy Saturday and Easter Day, but above all the Easter Vigil itself, should touch something elemental to human experience. For it is after all being used to express the movement from death to life, from darkness to light – the transformation of the cold and darkness of a stone tomb to the light and warmth of the resurrection. It is nothing less than the passage from the old life to new life in the risen Christ. St Augustine said that the Easter Vigil was 'the mother of all vigils'. It uses drama and storytelling, silence and song, a night of darkness and of light. It uses the images of light and dark, of fire and of water. It involves all the senses, sound and sight, taste, smell and touch. It is a shared experience, not least in listening to the retelling of a common story. But it remains essentially personal and private, something unique to each one of us.

It is only comparatively recently, in 1955, that the Easter Vigil was restored by Pope Pius XII, bringing back into the life of the Church something that is probably the oldest feature of the Easter celebration but one that has since then become increasingly widespread. From earliest times the Church would keep watch through the night and meditate on the mighty works of God as people heard the reading of key passages telling of his saving love, and joined in the saying of the psalms. It is a long night; a night of listening and of waiting, for any good storytelling that recalls the past cannot be hurried. At the greeting on this most holy night we the faithful are reminded that this is the Passover of the Lord and that by hearing his word and celebrating his mysteries we too may be confident that we shall share Christ's victory over death and with him pass from death to life.

All are encouraged to 'partake with gladness from this fair and radiant feast'. The opening sentence of the paschal homily of St John Chrysostom brings an invitation from a master who is generous in welcoming the latecomers and those who have delayed equally with those who have been faithful and have laboured long.

Enter then, all of you, into the joy of our Lord.
First and last, receive alike your reward.
Rich and poor, dance together.
You who have fasted and you who have not fasted,
Rejoice today.
. . .
Let none lament their poverty;
for the universal Kingdom is revealed.
Let none bewail their transgressions;
for the light of forgiveness has risen from the tomb.
Let none fear death;
for the death of the Saviour has set us free.

With the Paschal Candle lit, and tapers held by the congregation lit from it, comes the Exsultet, the Easter proclamation. It is always sung, by the light of these candles, for there is no way that this text can be simply read – it demands song. Heard only once in the year, in this solemn setting, we wait for those amazing opening words:

Rejoice, now, heavenly hosts and choirs of angels,
and let your trumpets sound salvation for the vict'ry of our
    mighty King.

Rejoice and sing now, all the round earth,
bright with a glorious splendour,
for darkness has been vanquished by our eternal King.

So now at last with the full image of death–resurrection established comes the moment for the renewal of baptism. The readings have included the passage from Romans where St Paul has told us that, just as Christ died and rose for us, so we are called to die and rise with him. We enter into this great mystery through the waters of baptism, which is at the heart of this night. Water is poured into the font, and the Paschal Candle is held above it; then it is plunged three times into the water while the priest asks for its blessing, and continues, 'May all who are buried with Christ in the death of baptism rise also with him to newness of life.' Now come the questions about the rejection of evil, the repentance of sins, the affirmation of faith. The successive responses are made so directly: I turn to Christ; I submit to Christ; I come to Christ; I believe and trust in him. And then finally, no longer personal but corporate, the last ringing declaration: 'This is the faith of the church. This is our faith.' Then, as the procession returns from the font to the altar, the congregation is sprinkled with holy water.

The vigil concludes with the celebration of the Eucharist. But of course we cannot say that it ends. It is now up to us to pray that this work of renewal will continue, deepening and enriching our baptismal vocation as we attempt to follow Christ on the path of daily discipleship.

Recovering Our
Historical Roots

'It is only by looking back that we have a future.' These words concluded a lecture on the preservation of museum objects by a conservationist who had been talking about the basements and storerooms below ground, that hidden part of the life of museums and galleries that few people see since they are out of sight of the public eye. I thought what a good analogy that gave for the role played by the past as the hidden foundation on which everything else depends but of which it is often only too easy to remain unaware. This book depends on 'a deep look at the deep past' – a phrase used by someone to explain what had drawn her to study early monasticism. 'Neglect of the past impoverishes our lives and without it we lack perspective and rootedness; something shrivels in us when we live only in the present.'[18] The idea can be taken even further if we see the dispossession of historical identity as an attribute of poverty. 'Those who inherit confront the world with a confident eye for they know that they have "a place in the scheme of things". The future, too, is theirs to claim.'[19]

Knowing that they had a place in the scheme of things for the early Church Fathers, together with the first monastic writers, and Benedict by the sixth century, meant that in their writing they naturally built on those who had gone before. In effect they are saying to their disciples: 'These words are not mine, but have come from inspired sources. I am not going to instruct you with a new teaching but with one that I have learned from my fathers.'[20] They saw themselves as the recipients of a tradition, which they would enrich with their own peculiar emphasis, and re-express in terms that reflected their personalities or those whom they were addressing. They entered into a rich and comprehensive tradition which they saw as common property, over which there was no sense of literary ownership. It is an entirely different literary scene from that of today where writers are protective, often combative, over rights, and regard plagiarism or the infringement of copyright as a most heinous offence. But here Christian learning and understanding is collected, assimilated and shared, transmitted to one another and to succeeding generations. The picture is one of confluence, of flowing together and mingling. Profoundly conscious of being the heirs of the past they felt a responsibility to propagate the wisdom accumulated by their predecessors and to hand it on to future generations.

This was a process that demanded creative skill, as we can see in the case of Benedict who had first read widely and then selected and unified, choosing what to bring together from a number of different sources. From this process has come that flexibility and generosity of spirit that is part of his genius, something that he wanted to transmit to his disciples. At the very end of the Rule, almost as his final word, comes a plea to his followers to read further from diverse sources, and to explore writers with differing backgrounds: on one hand the hermit tradition of those living alone, on the other the coenobitic tradition of those living in community.[21] This same openness is shown in the way in which he handles the biblical texts that form such an important part in his writing. Look, for example, at two paragraphs of the Prologue, verses 14–34, and we can see how he uses his quotations as a weaver would use different threads to create a beautifully variegated tapestry. Words coming from very different sources are presented, glossed and connected in order to flow together easily. He makes a seamless robe out of Thessalonians, the Psalms, Isaiah, Corinthians – so that it becomes a sequence which tells us that it is the Lord who is speaking uniformly throughout, and a saying from the Sermon on the Mount sums it all up. We are watching a man who brings his own humanity, his particular insight, to the handling of his sources and it is impossible to read the Rule without being aware of the freshness and excitement of his own voice, his personal charisma breaking through.

My own experience as a historian has also been drawn from diverse sources. What I have learnt has not come only from the written word but also from visual evidence, from particular landscapes and buildings that are a reflection of a way of life. I had the good fortune to live much of my life surrounded by the presence of the past in a way that demanded attention, and as a result I came to see the non-verbal as a form of text. My earliest childhood years were spent in Shropshire where my father was the vicar of a rural parish church that had been the site of a Benedictine priory in the Middle Ages, which meant I could see the monastic gatehouse from my bedroom window, and I knew the names of the priors who had preceded my father there in the Middle Ages. Later, in the ten years that I spent in Canterbury, I found myself at the heart of one of the greatest of all the European Benedictine communities, and I lived under the shadow of the monastic church that is now Canterbury Cathedral, the mother church of the worldwide Anglican Communion. In recent years I have returned to the Welsh borders, to a cottage which is only a few miles from one of the earliest Cistercian settlements, the abbey of Dore founded in 1147, which is unique in having been restored after the Reformation and having become the

Anglican parish church when the landowner Lord Scudamore rebuilt the choir for local parochial use.

Each of these places spells out a message for anyone who cares to read it: we revere and honour the past, but we do not see these as dead and fossilized stones – they are living stones carrying the past into the future, responding to the new demands and expectations of succeeding centuries. We need to be loyal to the past but we must not be encumbered by it, as Michael Mayne, the former Dean of Westminster Abbey, said. It is echoed in words from David Hodges, a member of the Cistercian community on Caldey Island in South Wales, who speaks of 'a process of creative fidelity to the tradition'. Loyalty to the past calls for the discernment to recognize what is of permanent value, and then see how it can be translated into terms that will touch contemporary life. This asks for a delicate balance between rootedness and openness, something that the monastic tradition understands.

If history gives us a place to stand, a sense of being earthed and grounded, this is not to be confused with being static. The Benedictine vows illustrate this well when they establish the paradox of keeping stability in tension with *conversatio morum*, which is roughly translated as the commitment to change, to the ongoing journey and whatever may lie ahead. It is thus a question of holding the balance. While we need the past we must not let ourselves become imprisoned by it or allow it to become an idol. Martin Smith expresses this well when he sets out the issue:

> faithfulness to tradition does not mean mere perpetuation or copying of ways from the past but a creative recovery of the past as a source of inspiration and guidance in our faithfulness to God's future.

Martin Smith was then the superior of the Cowley Fathers in the United States, the first Anglican community to be founded in England since the Reformation. When the American brothers decided to revise their rule they saw it as 'an expression of confidence in the living continuity of tradition, an act of inner appropriation and rearticulation'.[22]

It seems to me that we all need more and more to deepen the grasp that we have of our rich monastic heritage, and the closer we get to the source, the more fruitful and splendid our lives will be, in all kinds of varied expressions and manifestations . . . We have not scratched the surface of this rich land of ours that our Fathers have left us.[23]

These words come from a letter Thomas Merton wrote to a fellow monk, the Benedictine Fr Ronald Beloff. Merton has come to see the Fathers of the Church as friends, whom he knew well, for he was a skilled linguist and could read and study them in the original. The copy of the great patristic collection, Migne's *Patrologia*, in the library at Gethsemane with his annotations, shows us how he had soaked himself in their writings, while the tapes of the lectures that he gave to the novices show how he wished that the same might be true of them. He acknowledged that this was the basis of his life after he entered the monastery, and that it was this living tradition that formed and shaped him.

He believed that lives touched by contact with the riches of this glorious monastic heritage would become 'more fruitful and splendid' and his books opened that up so that the monastic tradition touched many people for whom it had hitherto been a well-kept secret. Others followed and a fellow Trappist spoke of 'cracking open the monastic treasury so that others in the Church might blessedly loot its contents'. Francis Kline then said that as the riches of the monastic tradition were made more available to the Church this became a two-way process, and in return monastics gained new energy from looking to the baptized 'who discern in the monastic way their own journey'.[24]

Merton continued to study seriously throughout his life, and in those later years when he was living in his hermitage he made a note in his journal, on Easter Monday, 19 April 1965: 'Study of medieval exegesis is a way of entering into the Christian experience of that age, an experience most relevant to us, for if we neglect it we neglect part of our totality.' But then he warns, and of course in his note-books he is writing to himself, that it must not be studied from the outside: 'my own vocation demands that it must be a deepened and experiential study from within'. He was speaking of his monastic vocation, but these are words that any of us can apply to our own baptismal vocation.

The voice of the past can and must speak. Of course we live in the present moment, but that does not entail the dismissal of the past. There is a danger of succumbing to the tyranny of living in the moment, entering 'the portals of the eternal present', to the loss of what has gone before. On the first page of *The Power of Now*, the author declares, 'I have little use for the past and rarely think about it,' although he is quite ready to tell his own story, ready to take us back to his earliest years in order to show us how he became 'a spiritual teacher'.[25] In contrast to this sort of storytelling, which is highly personal experience, when the Israelites told the stories of the years in the desert, the escape from Egypt and the feast of the Passover, it was to bring a sense of a shared past, a common identity – one to which we listen at the Easter Vigil. The Chief Rabbi, Jonathan Sachs, speaking on the radio just before the time of the Passover, said how important it was 'to tell and to retell stories that unite us and bring us hope'. And then he went on to say that this telling of sacred stories will naturally attract to itself a ritual, 'the ritual artistry of drama and symbol', and thus it becomes a point of reference for the way in which people conceptualize their lives.[26]

The Easter story, told in those early days, as people struggled to make sense of it – and as the newly baptized would hear it at the end of the Easter Vigil – would have made demands both on those who told it and on those who heard it. For as Rowan Williams put it in a recent article for a national newspaper that appeared on Holy Saturday:

> The untidy character of the stories leaves the reader or listener with work to do. Whatever else this is, it isn't the account of an event happening just to someone else in the past. It tells you that something in the world has opened up . . . Stories may have to be interrupted and questioned – they may mean that familiar things and persons have to be looked at with a new depth of attention.[27]

Each one of us hears and responds differently, even though we might be members of a large gathering, such as one of the ceremonies of the Triduum. Recognizing this, and realizing that there might be social and racial tensions among his hearers, St Gregory of Nazianzus showed in his vivid retelling of the story of the passion and the resurrection how something different is asked of each one of us:

> If you are Simon of Cyrene, take up the cross and follow.
> If you are crucified with him as a robber, have the honesty to acknowledge God.
> If you are Joseph of Arimathea, ask the executioner for the body.
> If you are Nicodemus, the man who served God by night, prepare him for burial with perfumes,
> If you are one or other Mary, or Salome, or Joanna, shed tears in the early morning. Be the first to see the stone removed, and perhaps the angels too, and even Jesus himself.[28]

In earlier times, when tradition was handed on by word of mouth from one generation to another, the corporate aspect of tradition would have been entirely natural and unselfconscious. In 1905, an old woman called Janet MacLeod, on the island of Eigg, off the west coast of Scotland, when asked where she had heard a particular song, replied:

> I heard it from many a person . . . My father's people were famous for old songs . . . When my father came to Trotternish, whether or not he brought any property with him, he at least brought enough poetry and lore to fill the world . . . was it not said about them that they never forgot any poetry or lore, but were constantly adding to the cairn . . .

The pile of stones to which everyone adds one more stone is not a bad way to describe this accumulated legacy which was of more value than gold or property. Everything that endures is good.

> Shared gold goes not far,
> But a shared song lasts a long time.[29]

Here we hear directly from someone who has the sense of continuity with the past and who recognizes what that brought to their lives.

I would like to think something of that same sense of giving and taking could apply when I come to reading voices from the past. If I think of myself as having a conversation with a written text just as I would have a conversation with a living person it is good to remember what a long history 'the art of conversation' has had in the Church. Conversations guided by the Holy Spirit, between an elder and a disciple, between the abba or the amma, dating back to the earliest times in the desert and those who came to learn from them, have always played an important role in the teachings and the spread of the faith. It is an art that takes many forms, not only between master and pupil but between equals and friends, or, as in the case of Benedict and Scholastica, between brother and sister.

St Aelred, the twelfth-century Cistercian Abbot of Rievaulx, said that whenever he was talking with a friend there was always a third person present and that was Christ. Perhaps we should think of good conversation as an art form which demands as much of us as other skills and interests. This means a willingness to listen fully and to take time. At the start this may ask for quite a lot of confidence and openness. It is good to remember that, like digging for gold, the insights we receive will be in direct proportion to efforts to listen patiently, and to wait. It has many parallels with talking to someone from another culture or background who will be bringing with them all their baggage of history and tradition, of suffering and triumph. I cannot really meet them until I am willing to be open and honest about where I stand and what my own story is. There is much here in common with the art of hospitality as the Rule shows it to us: the need to be reciprocal, to receive as well as to give, and above all the need to show reverence and respect for the other.

The words that I found at the door of a convent in Zimbabwe express this well. Since they were given no attribution I have no idea where they might come from, but in the situation of a strife-ridden country they made a forceful impact on me:

My first task in approaching another people,
another culture,
is to take off my shoes.
For the place that I am approaching is holy.
Otherwise I may find myself
treading on another's dreams,
their memories, their stories.
More serious still – I might forget
that God was there . . .

When St Gregory wrote his life of Benedict in the form of a dialogue he introduced the figure of Peter the deacon who interrupts and questions, asking for clarification. He is a young man who needs to stop and think things out before he can take the next step since he cannot move on while there is still confusion in his mind. I find this a useful analogy for approaching an original text (such as those, for example, included in the Anthology of this book). If I picture myself having an interior dialogue with what I am reading, I will debate and discuss, almost as though this is a living encounter between friends, teacher and disciple. This can be particularly valuable in cases where the voice is not always crystal clear – for, to return to an earlier theme, I must be prepared to discern and to welcome truth in various expressions and there may well be ambiguity and paradox in the way in which the words touch us all differently.

It is only too attractive to escape the demands of reading in this way, and to become selective or to make the past too easily accessible by looking for what we hope to find. What has happened with the enthusiasm for 'the Celtic Church' shows the dangers of popularizing and trivialization (the anamchara is seen as soul friend, but taken out of the context of the penitentials). I was surprised, and pleased, when I happened to reread something that I had written in 1986, in the introduction to a small book that was in some ways a pioneer in this field:

> To discover a tradition just because we need it can be a dangerous undertaking. It is vital to be strictly honest here and not to lapse into any sentimentality or romanticism which will merely find in the Celtic world material to feed contemporary needs and longings, and thus to remake the past in our own image . . .[30]

When Patrick Barry tells us that we should approach the Rule of St Benedict as 'a still-living text' I think that that should also apply to much of the material of the past. Here are ancient texts, having a history that is old 'but still living and breaking forth into new perspectives'. We should of course, as far as we can, put it into context and try to see what it meant for its time, but also see how it can still carry significance for today's very different world. If we stay with it, and try to penetrate its hidden depths, we will find that 'it opens up to us new facets of our inner being and reveals new meaning in our lives'.[31]

Recovering Our Symbolic Identity

'Human minds and human words are altogether unequal to the grandeur of the things I have to talk to you about.'[32] A modern rendering of the baptismal teachings of Theodore sets the key for the discussion of the role that image and symbol, the visual, played in baptism in the early centuries. From time immemorial symbols have played a vital role, for, as Mircea Eliade, one of the best known authorities on the subject, reminds us, 'symbols never disappear from the reality of the psyche'.[33] As a result, the making of symbols is one of the most characteristic of all human activities, and above all where religion is concerned. In a letter to Mark van Doren, an old friend from Colombia days, Thomas Merton wrote:

The earliest Fathers knew that all things, as such, are symbolic by their very being and nature, and all talk of something beyond themselves. Their meaning is not something we impose upon them but a mystery which we can discover in them if we have the eyes to look with.[34]

The Greek word symbol means 'thrown together', so it is hardly surprising to find symbols lending themselves to multiple layers of meaning. We should expect symbols to appeal to more than one faculty of the human person, and to reflect the many levels on which we live. A symbol is not an end in itself – it is a call to a reality beyond the rational, a representation of something not explicable in words. The architect and garden designer Charles Jencks says that 'a symbol is meant to mediate between everyday existence and eternity, and therefore has several related meanings which unite the two.'[35]

The theme at the biennial convention of the American Benedictine Academy held in 1994 was 'Creating a Renewed Monastic Environment: Symbol, Ritual and Practice', an occasion at which artists and scholars blended their wisdom with the experience of the Benedictine monastic tradition. Their hope was that they might enter 'more deeply and intuitively into the symbolic level of our identity'.[36] The papers might seem to be specifically aimed at monastics, but as always, monasticism tells us much about the fullness and the fulfilment of our own humanity. What Terrence Kardong has to say about symbol and ritual in the Rule of St Benedict applies to any of us:

Successful symbols always speak to the heart as well as the mind, and they also engage the will toward action. In addition symbol seems particularly capable of reaching the human subconscious. Given these potentialities, the symbol is a staple of all forms of art. It is probably the most powerful and influential form of communication.[37]

This is something that Bonnie Thurston, being both a poet and a theologian, recognizes:

> It is crucially important that Christians understand metaphorical or symbolic language. It is the primary way in which human beings can speak of God and the primary way in which God speaks to human beings. Through the mystery of inspiration, God empowered the biblical writers to make God known by way of human language. The metaphors and symbols they used carry us from the known to the Unknown, the word carries us to the Word. Moreover, as metaphor and symbol, they speak to the whole person, not just to part of the person, and this reflects God's plan and providence. Metaphorical and symbolic language engages emotions and intellect, heart and head, and, if Jung is correct, a deep connectedness uniting the whole human family.[38]

Image and symbol become a way into reality that brings a welcome relief from the cascade of words that daily and insistently ambush us on all sides. For while words batter us, symbols are gentle, pleasing. They carry 'aesthetic truth', for in the first instance they are a source of joy and delight. But they are also there to work for us, bringing nourishment and energy to the inner life. They are not dogmatic, they do not deal in definition and precision, yet because they touch the subconscious they address the heart and mind and energize the will. They also hold layers of meaning, mysteries which reveal themselves – or are dug out – with time and attention. A symbol should 'go on deepening'.[39] In this telling phrase Flannery O'Connor is reminding us that a symbol has the power not only to reveal the hitherto unknown, but also to call us forward, and invite us to participate in something beyond itself.

Nicodemus, a cautious man, came to Jesus by night, addressing him as master, and hoping for answers to his questions. But he was not given what he was looking for. The response came instead in the form of an image that baffled him. Being told about being born again was not what he had expected to hear. Instead he was challenged to open up to mystery. He then disappears from view, but when we meet up with him again much later in the Gospel he is a changed man, not a seeker but a disciple. This is one of the characteristics of an image: it takes time to work. This is typical of how Jesus taught. If we think about the pattern of his teaching in his lifetime we find that it was never declaratory or didactic. He did not want to make people look to him for nice, safe answers. He did not lay down ethical rules or statements. He was concerned – as was Benedict – to shape the attitude, 'the disposition of the heart', to lead us to the depths where our God-given life is attempting to grow.[40]

Jesus taught by parables and stories, which touched his hearers and left them to make the connection with their own lives – even though that might not always happen immediately. When he used them as tools of instruction it was not in order to present regulations or behavioural norms. Dominic Crossan reminds us that parables are full of silence; they ask us to sit with them, and to take time, for we shall not easily exhaust their meaning. This frightens us:

> The parables of Jesus seek to draw one into the Kingdom, and they challenge us to act and to live from the gift that is experienced therein. But we do not want parables. We want precepts and we want programs . . . We are frightened of the lonely silences within the parables.[41]

Luci Shaw, a poet, reminds us of the biblical use of storytelling and parable, poetry and image, visions and dreams, rather than the abstract or doctrinal statement:

> Imagination and metaphor, the making of truth or story into verbal pictures rather than abstract prose statements, is the methodology consistently called upon in the imagery of the Bible – the teaching tool on which God has set the imprint of approval by constant use.[42]

The challenge to enter more deeply and intuitively into the symbolic level of our identity is at odds with a society which likes to assess, measure, analyse. We are far removed from a world alive with symbolic meaning, one in which moreover one symbol does not displace another.[43] The symbolic world of earlier centuries is one from which we are now almost entirely alienated, though I believe that we need to recapture it if we are to enter into the riches of early Christian teaching, and in particular the teachings given in preparation for baptism, and the rite of baptism itself.

This was known to the Syrian St Ephrem as a beautiful and mysterious truth :

Lord, your symbols are everywhere
yet You are hidden from everywhere;
though Your symbol is on high
yet the height does not perceive that You are;
though Your symbol is in the depth,
it does not comprehend who You are;
though your Symbol is in the sea,
though Your symbol is on dry land,
it is not aware what You are,
Blessed is the Hidden One shining out![44]

When the community of St John's Collegeville in Minnesota embarked upon their great project of commissioning some of the very finest modern calligraphy to create the first handwritten Bible for five hundred years the abbot spoke of it as an exercise 'in the retrieval of the imagination'. They envisioned a Bible that would ignite the spiritual imagination of people for centuries to come. The abbot explained what underlay the community's vision:

It comes alive, and not least for the young. The Word becomes sacramental. It is not just a text. It is like the Eucharist: a visual image of the Word.

He said that his hope was that as the Bible moved around the world and was shown in exhibitions it would encourage people to pore over it, taking time, finding themselves encountering the Scriptures in a fresh way, finding 'new exciting things'.[45]

Much of what I have been saying here shows the importance of 'taking time', words used by Abbot John Klassen. Rowan Williams, in a significantly titled lecture 'New Words for God', speaks of *unveiling*, a word which suggests a gentle, slow approach, taking time to read, digest, ponder:

> When we move with poetry and the imagination, when we deal with symbols and images, we become people who are happy with mystery, and open to discovery . . . To deepen mystery, to embrace complexity is risky. We have to have courage enough to be ready for an unveiling which can be a startling process.[46]

Thomas Merton, who was himself a poet and an artist as well as a Trappist monk, was always insistent on the importance of the imagination which he called 'a discovering faculty, a faculty for seeing relationships, for seeing meanings that are special and even quite new . . .'.[47] Both his parents were artists, and although he had a gift for calligraphy and sketches, his skill as an artist is really best seen in his photography which tells us much about how he brought a contemplative and artistic eye to the world around him. Writing in the 1960s, in his hermitage years, in an era in which the spiritual imagination was 'impotent, sterile, or dead', he feared that what would follow was violence, destruction and chaos. It is perhaps significant that his thesis had been on William Blake, a man for whom the creative and religious imagination played an extremely important part, saying that it was the faculty by which men and women penetrated ultimate reality and religious mystery.

In his introduction to *Religion in Wood*, his work on Shaker furniture,[48] Merton quoted Blake's rhetorical question 'Why is the Bible more entertaining and instructive than any other book? Is it not because they [*sic*] are addressed to the imagination, which is spiritual sensation, and not mediate to the understanding or reason?'

Merton tells us that in the creation God has given us a world which is sacramental, and we should look at it with 'rinsed eyes'. (Perhaps we should take those words and say 'baptized eyes'.) We do not need to launch a search for new symbols or new symbol-making; instead, we should be taking more time to see the symbols that surround us, and allow them to yield up their full riches. Sr Bede Luetkemeyer says that 'the way of symbols is to awaken us to the discovery of the God-dimension present in all things', and this call to recognize all as symbol is a call to 'the deeper realms of faith, a call to see the world with clear eyes; the clearer the eye the more the symbol becomes visible, and the more individual symbols become meaningful'. But she warns us not to forget that they are merely the outward garb. They do not exist for their own sakes; they point beyond themselves to 'the simple marvellous, transcendent truth of the symbols'.[49]

This is important if we are to appreciate what the saying of the creed meant to the catechumens. In the early Church the creeds were known as 'Symbols', which should not surprise us since 'all talk of God is through symbols'.[50] Thus at baptism they were reciting something originally created to summarize for them what the Christian life is committing them to, but it cannot be the whole picture. Creeds should be seen more as pointers to exploration, or, in the words of Martin Smith, 'a constellation of metaphors and images all crying out for interpretation'. He then goes on to elaborate this with the analogy of seeing the symbol as a token or counter like the stub of a theatre ticket, which is not the performance itself but will take us to where the performance is. 'The creeds were originally created to summarise for converts what baptism was going to let them into. Reciting the baptismal symbol they were admitted to the drama.'

If we are willing to be taken into the realms of the imagination, and of poetic insight, we might find it a dangerous even a risky undertaking. But it does not involve the escape from reality; rather, it means entering into the deeper realities to which these symbols are pointing us, whether within ourselves or in the world around us. What will it ask of us? Are we ready for this encounter? For the unfolding of these mysteries that are close at hand but still hidden? And then, having listened and having gazed deeply, are we prepared to respond to what we will find?

The River of Grace

'Baptism, whether ancient or modern, is the hinge upon which Christian identity turns.'[51] In the Lent course that he gave in the church in Jerusalem about the year 350, St Cyril declared: 'Jesus sanctified baptism when he himself was baptised . . . He was baptised in order that he might impart grace and dignity to those who receive the sacrament.' The scene in the river Jordan was never far from mind.[52] What the Red Sea was for the people of Israel, the Jordan was for the Christians.

> Hasten, O man, to my Jordan,
> John is not calling but Christ.
> For the river of grace is running everywhere.[53]

How is it possible to recapture what baptism, that 'river of grace', meant in the first five centuries of the Church? Is it still possible to enter into the anticipation and the excitement felt by those men and women accepted for baptism as the actual moment grew closer? The preparation would have begun months, often years, beforehand, making it even more serious and momentous. By the fourth century, when Easter had become accepted as the normal time for baptism, those who wished to become candidates were urged to 'give in their names' (a phrase which became the technical term for a request for baptism) at the start of Lent.

In the account that Egeria, the nun from Southern Gaul or Spain, wrote for her sisters of her experience on pilgrimage to Jerusalem at the end of the fourth century, she describes the lights, the incense, the processions, the singing that she saw:

> Those who give in their names do so the day before Lent begins; the presbyter writes down the names of all of them . . . Later, on another day in Lent, the bishop's chair is set up in the middle of the great church . . . Then the candidates are brought in one by one, the men with their 'fathers', the women with their 'mothers' [i.e. their sponsors]. Then the bishop asks their neighbours: 'Is he a good-living man? Does he respect his parents?'[54]

The list of questions was long but if the answers were satisfactory the bishop would 'write down the candidate's name with his own hand' which counted as enrolment, and they were now catechumens, that is, under instruction. Chrysostom reminded them that the name 'catechumen' was derived from the Greek word 'echo' and that what they heard was intended not only for their ears, but should resonate in their minds and find expression in their lives.[55]

In the earliest days the requirement of faith in the message of the gospel, repentance and the acceptance of Christian morality were not secured by any formal arrangements. But from about the middle of the second century we get a glimpse of what was done to prepare candidates both in doctrinal understanding and moral conduct, above all in prayer and fasting, while by the third century the time of preparation normally lasted for three years, a kind of novitiate in which they were trained in the practices of the Christian life.

At the end of the time the catechumens were again examined about their moral conduct, and if this proved acceptable they could then proceed to the proximate preparation which took place in the weeks before Easter. This was teaching which gave full scope to drama, symbol and imagery, for it dealt with fundamental issues in all human experience: life and death, slavery and freedom. As the time of Easter drew closer so the sense of urgency and excitement grew, for this is nothing less than the movement from a life of servitude and death to the new life in Christ.

The rite of baptism itself began at three o'clock on the afternoon of Good Friday and as those about to be baptized filed into the vestibule or forecourt of the baptistery they could not fail to be aware of the significance of the hour. For now finally the night has come, the long-awaited moment. As each one knelt down in turn St John Chrysostom (who lived from 347 to 407, mainly in Antioch) reminded them that they were at the foot of the cross. It was therefore with the figure of the crucified Christ in their minds that they then turned to face the west to make their renunciation of Satan: 'I abjure Satan, and all his angels, and all his service, and all his deceptions, and all his worldly glamour . . .'[56] They had been told many times of the guile of the evil one who would pursue them even to the font itself: 'the devil, bold and shameless, the source of all evil, will follow you up to the waters of salvation'. They knew that they must meet him face to face in combat in order to break his power. Kneeling, with hands outstretched, 'the posture of one who prays' as Theodore of Mopsuestia (probably in his lectures during his episcopate 392–428), told them, and with their gaze directed to heaven, each in turn was asked by the bishop to make a personal act of renunciation of Satan and a profession of allegiance to Christ. The physical stance indicated the interior disposition:

> You offer prayer to God,
> and implore Him to grant you deliverance
> and participation in the heavenly benefits.

The words with which they addressed Satan were clear and strong, and it was almost as though he were immediately before them:

> I renounce you, Satan . . . I no longer fear your power . . . For Christ has dissolved that power . . . I renounce you, you cunning and most vicious serpent. I renounce you, you plotter, who under the guise of friendship have worked all manner of wrong and caused our first parents to secede from God. I renounce you, Satan, author and associate in every evil.[57]

Since the west was regarded as the region of visible darkness, and because Satan who had darkness as his lot had his empire in darkness, they turned to face westward for this act of renunciation. Then in contrast, when they turned towards the east, they were facing towards Christ, the Lord of light and life, who by his own death had trampled down darkness and death. Cyril told them of the promise that there 'God's Paradise opens before you, that Eden . . . The place of light, that garden which God planted in the east.'[58]

Confessing to the absolute rule of Christ, and rejoicing in their deliverance from slavery to Satan, it was as though the miracle of the Exodus story was repeated – but on a greater scale, as John Chrysostom told them:

> The Jews saw miracles. Now you shall see greater and much more brilliant ones than those seen when the Jews went forth from Egypt. You did not see the Pharaohs and his armies drowned, but you did see the drowning of the devil and his armies. The Jews passed through the sea; you have passed through the sea of death. They were delivered from the Egyptians; you are set free from the demon. They put aside their servitude to barbarians; you have set aside the far more hazardous servitude to sin.[59]

They knew that even though there would be struggle, perhaps face-to-face encounter, victory was ensured. They will overcome Satan, they will hear words that are an elaboration of the message of the angel to Cornelius from Acts 10.4:

God has looked upon your tribulation which you were pre-
viously undergoing and has mercy upon you because you were
for a long time captives of the tyrant and served a cruel servitude
to him. He saw the number and nature of the calamities which
you have endured, and this moved him to deliver you from that
servitude and from the great number of ancient tribulations, and
to bring you to freedom and to grant you to participate in the
ineffable heavenly benefits.[60]

And now came the first of the anointings which were so significant
in any early baptismal rite, for as they thought of Christ rising out
of the waters of the Jordan they thought of him as the Anointed
One, anointed by the Spirit: 'The Spirit of the Lord is upon me
because he has anointed me . . .'

The oil was pure olive oil, blessed, empowered by the Spirit and
thus brought into the realm of the sacred, so that in turn it could
become a vehicle for sanctification. Hippolytus tells us that just
before the time of baptism the bishop would 'give thanks', that is to
say, he would bless oil with these words:

> O Lord, may you in blessing this oil,
> give holiness to those who are anointed with it
> and to those who receive it,
> this oil with which you have anointed kings and priests and
>   prophets.[61]

This first anointing (since the actual number varied according to
different rites and different places) is with the oil of exorcism when,
by their renunciation of Satan, the candidates have changed their
allegiance.

The marking of the forehead with the cross was a sealing of the
contract that they now belonged to Christ; the sign that they had

been chosen as combatants to serve under him. They entered the spiritual arena as athletes, needing all their strength for the conflict that lay ahead. Chrysostom taught them that this cross guaranteed their victory, for the mark they were now carrying radiated a power 'in order that the enemy may turn away his eyes. For he dare not look you in the face when he sees the lightning flash which leaps forth from it and blinds his eyes':

> It is for this reason that the bishop anoints you on your forehead and marks you with the seal to make the devil turn away his eyes. He does not dare to look at you directly because he sees the light blazing from your head and blinding his eyes.[62]

The second anointing took place immediately before the actual baptism itself on Holy Saturday night. In the darkness of the night they divested themselves of their clothes so that their entirely naked body, from their hair to their feet, could be anointed 'with the olive oil of the spirit'. This stripping is a symbolic gesture at many levels, most obviously the peeling off of the garments and with them the evil deeds of the old self also. But there is also Christ's own stripping at the crucifixion, and his nakedness on the cross where what was meant to be humiliation becomes victory. At its most profound level it was a symbolic stripping away of the many layers of self-deception so that all the carefully constructed defences and masks would be taken down and the essential truth of the self laid bare. And finally, as they are now led to the water, there is a further image, for by picturing the baptismal pool as a symbol of the garden of Paradise there is a suggestion of the return to primeval innocence. 'Marvellous!' Cyril addresses them with Genesis 2 in mind. 'You were naked in the sight of all and were not ashamed! Truly you bore the image of the first formed Adam, who was naked in the garden and "was not ashamed".'[63]

At this point the doors of the baptistery were thrown wide open. There must have been a loud sound as they were drawn back, and there was the blaze of colour and light, in stark contrast to the semi-darkness of the vestibule. The bishop led the way and the catechumens followed with the presbyters, the deacons and deaconesses, and the sponsors. They entered what must have seemed like a brilliant pavilion, with mosaic decorations and lights. Here in effect they came face to face with what that symbolic turning to the east had promised: 'the gate of the bright meadow of Paradise'.[64] A paschal homily describes the scene:

> On this feast the baptismal font, the womb which begets pure life, is ablaze with the light of candles under the cross, the tree of faith.[65]

The distinguished Benedictine monk and liturgical scholar Aidan Kavanagh helps us to picture it and the many levels of symbolism that it carried:

> It is warm and humid, and it glows. It is a golden paradise in a bathhouse, in a mausoleum, an oasis, Eden restored: the navel of the world, where death and life meet, copulate and become indistinguishable from each other.[66]

The first one to enter the baptismal pool was led down by a deacon, into water that was warm (heated by a furnace), and as they did so the oil must have spread outwards, making iridescent patterns. Then came the question from the bishop: 'Do you believe in God?' Augustine had described baptism as the 'sacrament of faith'. Standing there in the pool each one replies, making their confession of Christian faith. It has been a long journey that has led up to this moment, the central moment of the baptismal rite. Perhaps they had learnt the creed orally, article by article, when it was still too dangerous to write it down; perhaps they had made a public profession in the presence of the assembled congregation the previous

Sunday. But now it is their own personal responsibility. Each had now to respond in turn to this question, and after each answered 'Yes' the deacon firmly pushed the head into the water until it was fully immersed. This was repeated three times, with the deacon's hand resting on them and pressing them down under the water. 'Do you believe in Jesus Christ . . . ?' 'Do you believe in the Holy Spirit . . . ?' This is the moment to which all the long preparation has come: the affirmation of faith in the trinitarian God, Father, Son and Holy Spirit, to which the reply is firmly given: 'I believe.' And after the third time comes the declaration: 'You are baptised in the name of the Father, and of the Son, and of the Holy Spirit,' the trinitarian baptismal formula following the instruction given to the disciples, 'Go therefore and make disciples of all nations, baptizing them in the name of the Father and of the Son and of the Holy Spirit' (Matthew 28.19).

'Baptism is a burial and a resurrection.' Cyril puts it at its simplest. It lends itself to some of the very finest writing, and it must have been extraordinarily powerful to have heard the spoken word. We are fortunate that so much has come down to us, and that we can catch the feeling of the drama and the sense of the enormous significance of what was happening. 'In the same moment you were dying and being born, and that saving water was at once your grave and your mother.' There is nothing more inescapable than this, the mystery of life and death, death and life, and the freshness of tone of the homilies still rings out, a theme recalled time and again with awe and gratitude:

> What Solomon said in another context is apposite to you: 'There is a time to be born, and a time to die', but the opposite is true in your case – there is a time to die and a time to be born. A single moment achieves both ends, and your begetting was

simultaneous with your death. What a strange and astonishing situation. We did not really die, we were not really buried, we did not really hang from a cross and rise again. Our imitation was symbolic, because our salvation is a reality.[67]

Theodore writes in the first person singular which allows us to identify with what it must have meant to him:

> When at my baptism I plunge my head,
> I receive the death of Christ our Lord and desire to have his burial,
> and because of this I firmly believe in the resurrection of our Lord,
> and when I rise from the water, I think I have symbolically risen.[68]

Baptism not only cleansed from sin, and brought the gift of the Holy Spirit, 'it was also a counterpart of Christ's suffering'. The triple immersion was of course trinitarian but it was also seen as a re-enactment of the three days and nights that Christ spent in the tomb, in the depths of the earth. In the words of these early baptismal teachings:

> You submerged yourself three times in the water and emerged: by this symbolic action you were secretly re-enacting the burial of Christ three days in the tomb. Just as our saviour spent three days and nights in the womb of the earth, so you saw nothing when immersed as if it were night, but you emerged as if to the light of day. In one and the same action you died and were born; that water of salvation became both tomb and mother for you.

As each of the baptized left the pool, and their place was taken by another, they were welcomed and embraced by all present. They emerged naked, and were dressed not in the clothes that they had worn before, but in white. Replacing the clothes put aside before baptism, which symbolized the old person, they put on this white robe symbolic of putting on the new person. Whiteness stands for joy, and the quotation from Isaiah 61.10 comes in very aptly here: 'He has dressed me in the garment of salvation and with the robe of gladness he has clothed me.' This is a shining garment, a royal robe, a garment of immortality, and it might be the occasion for a hymn to be sung:

> Vouchsafe unto me the robe of light,
> O Thou who clothes Thyself with light as with a garment,
> Christ our God, plenteous in mercy.

But there were further associations, for white robes were also a symbol not only of the resurrection but also of the innocence which should now distinguish the newly baptized, and the purity and joy which lay ahead in the coming kingdom. Above all, they would think of the shining forth of Christ at the transfiguration when his robes became as white as snow. If the baptismal robe recalls the garments of the transfigured Christ it brings a reminder to the newly baptized that they now share in the glory of the risen Christ. Baptism is after all, as St Paul says, a putting on of Christ himself: 'all you who have been baptised into Christ have put on Christ'.

Finally there was the third and final anointing, this time with the oil of thanksgiving, the chrism or myron. This was olive oil, which was mixed with balsam to give it a fragrance, and Chrysostom pointed out that what the oil was for the athlete the myron was for the bride.

This anointing was sometimes called 'the aroma of Christ', or 'the scent of the knowledge of the gospel'. But Cyril went further with a play on the words 'Christ', 'Christian' and 'chrism', which allowed him to show that as a result of his or her anointing the newly baptized has become another Christ. It brought the sense of being about to go out into the world, with each separate part of the head – forehead, ears, nostrils – equipped and ready for their work in the world. 'I can do all things through [Christ] who strengthens me' (Philippians 4.13).

Then as each was given a burning terracotta oil lamp the new Christians would hear the Easter hymn ringing out:

> Christ is risen from the dead.
> He has crushed death by his death,
> And bestowed life on those who lay in the tomb.

While this was being sung the baptismal party would walk into what had now become the dawn, led by the bishop into the church, where as they enter they too take up the hymn 'Christ is risen ...'. The scene was one of rejoicing and delight, with colour and light, the table spread and the feast waiting. Chrysostom describes it for us:

> As soon as they came forth from those sacred waters, all who are present embrace them, greet them, kiss them, rejoice with them, and congratulate them, because those who were heretofore slaves and captives have suddenly become free men and sons and have been invited to the royal table. For straightaway after they come up from the waters, they are led to the awesome table heavy laden with countless flavours where they taste of the Master's body and blood, and become a dwelling place for the Holy Spirit.[69]

It became customary in the West for these new Christians to continue to wear their new white robes throughout the octave of Easter until the following Sunday, and it was called 'the shining week'.[70] For Chrysostom it was a wedding garment for a marriage-feast that lasted seven days. 'Since they have put on Christ himself, wherever they go they are like angels on earth, rivalling the brilliance of the rays of the sun.' Cyril saw it as

> The garment of light,
> a shining garment,
> a royal robe.

II

THE PROLOGUE

The Prologue

¹Listen carefully, my son, to the master's instructions, and attend to them with the ear of your heart. This is advice from a father who loves you; welcome it, and faithfully put it into practice. ²The labor of obedience will bring you back to him from whom you had drifted through the sloth of disobedience. ³This message of mine is for you, then, if you are ready to give up your own will, once and for all, and armed with the strong and noble weapons of obedience to do battle for the true King, Christ the Lord.

⁴First of all, every time you begin a good work, you must pray to him most earnestly to bring it to perfection. ⁵In his goodness, he has already counted us as his sons, and therefore we should never grieve him by our evil actions. ⁶With his good gifts which are in us, we must obey him at all times that he may never become the angry father who disinherits his sons, ⁷nor the dread lord, enraged by our sins, who punishes us forever as worthless servants for refusing to follow him to glory.

⁸Let us get up then, at long last, for the Scriptures rouse us when they say: *It is high time for us to arise from sleep* (Rom 13:11). ⁹Let us open our eyes to the light that comes from God, and our ears to the voice from heaven that every day calls out this charge: ¹⁰*If you hear his voice today, do not harden your hearts* (Ps 94[95]:8). ¹¹And again: *You that have ears to hear, listen to what the Spirit says to the churches* (Rev 2:7). ¹²And

what does he say? *Come and listen to me, sons; I will teach you the fear of the Lord* (Ps 33[34]:12). [13]*Run while you have the light* of life, *that the darkness* of death *may not overtake you* (John 12:35).

[14]Seeking his workman in a multitude of people, the Lord calls out to him and lifts his voice again: [15]*Is there anyone here who yearns for life and desires to see good days?* (Ps 33[34]:13) [16]If you hear this and your answer is "I do," God then directs these words to you: [17]If you desire true and eternal life, *keep your tongue free from vicious talk and your lips from all deceit; turn away from evil and do good; let peace be your quest and aim* (Ps 33[34]:14–15). [18]Once you have done this, my *eyes will be upon* you *and* my *ears will listen* for your *prayers; and even before you ask me, I will say* to you: *Here I am* (Isa 58:9). [19]What, dear brothers, is more delightful than this voice of the Lord calling to us? [20]See how the Lord in his love shows us the way of life. [21]Clothed then with faith and the performance of good works, let us set out on this way, with the Gospel for our guide, that we may deserve to see him *who has called* us *to his kingdom* (1 Thess 2:12).

[22]If we wish to dwell in the tent of this kingdom, we will never arrive unless we run there by doing good deeds. [23]But let us ask the Lord with the Prophet: *Who will dwell in your tent, Lord; who will find rest upon your holy mountain?* (Ps 14[15]:1) [24]After this question, brothers, let us listen well to what the Lord says in reply, for he shows us the way to his tent. [25]*One who walks without blemish,* he says, *and is just in all his dealings;* [26]*who speaks the truth from his heart and has not practiced deceit with his tongue;* [27]*who has not wronged a fellowman in any way, nor listened to slanders against his neighbor* (Ps 14[15]:2–3). [28]He has *foiled* the *evil one,* the devil, at every turn, flinging both him and his promptings far *from the sight* of his heart. While these temptations were still *young, he caught hold of them and dashed them against* Christ (Ps 14[15]:4; 136[137]:9). [29]These people *fear the Lord,*

and do not become elated over their good deeds; they judge it is the Lord's power, not their own, that brings about the good in them. [30]*They praise* (Ps 14[15]:4) the Lord working in them, and say with the Prophet: *Not to us, Lord, not to us give the glory, but to your name alone* (Ps 113[115:1]:9). [31]In just this way Paul the Apostle refused to take credit for the power of his preaching. He declared: *By God's grace I am what I am* (1 Cor 15:10). [32]And again he said: *He who boasts should make his boast in the Lord* (2 Cor 10:17). [33]That is why the Lord says in the Gospel: *Whoever hears these words of mine and does them is like a wise man who built his house upon rock;* [34]*the floods came and the winds blew and beat against the house, but it did not fall: it was founded on rock* (Matt 7:24–25).

[35]With this conclusion, the Lord waits for us daily to trans-late into action, as we should, his holy teachings. [36]Therefore our life span has been lengthened by way of a truce, that we may amend our misdeeds. [37]As the Apostle says: *Do you not know that the patience of God is leading you to repent* (Rom 2:4)? [38]And indeed the Lord assures us in his love: *I do not wish the death of the sinner, but that he turn back to me and live* (Ezek 33:11).

[39]Brothers, now that we have asked the Lord who will dwell in his tent, we have heard the instruction for dwelling in it, but only if we fulfill the obligations of those who live there. [40]We must, then, prepare our hearts and bodies for the battle of holy obedience to his instructions. [41]What is not possible to us by nature, let us ask the Lord to supply by the help of his grace. [42]If we wish to reach eternal life, even as we avoid the torments of hell, [43]then – while there is still time, while we are in this body and have time to accomplish all these things by the light of life – [44]we must run and do now what will profit us forever.

[45]Therefore we intend to establish a school for the Lord's service. [46]In drawing up its regulations, we hope to set down

nothing harsh, nothing burdensome. [47]The good of all concerned, however, may prompt us to a little strictness in order to amend faults and to safeguard love. [48]Do not be daunted immediately by fear and run away from the road that leads to salvation. It is bound to be narrow at the outset. [49]But as we progress in this way of life and in faith, we shall run on the path of God's commandments, our hearts overflowing with the inexpressible delight of love. [50]Never swerving from his instructions, then, but faithfully observing his teaching in the monastery until death, we shall through patience share in the sufferings of Christ that we may deserve also to share in his kingdom. Amen.

I love the Prologue. I return to it time and again, and each time find something new. It is ancient wisdom which, like the gospel, is always new. This means that it reveals fresh insights as one approaches it at successive times of one's life, from a different perspective or in a different context.[71] Here I am seeing the Prologue as a way into prayer, but in the context of its connection with the catechical instruction given in preparation for baptism. I have therefore looked at some of its underlying themes, using the text as a series of short reflections on what is involved in baptism and how I may deepen and strengthen my baptismal vocation.

The Rule is an epitome of scripture. In the Middle Ages it was common to speak of it as a digest of the gospel. Benedict is scriptural to the core. His mind and heart were totally shaped by the Bible.[72] He was a man soaked by the Word. In his final chapter he asks this rhetorical question: 'What page, what passage of the inspired books of the Old and New Testaments is not the truest of guides for human life?' (Chapter 73.3). This is particularly apparent in the Prologue: 'What is more delightful than this voice of the Lord calling to us?' The Scriptures are our guide (21), and the message comes over in a very immediate and urgent way as Benedict speaks of the Scriptures rousing us (8), calling out to us, inviting us (9).

We have no hope of discovering the full depths of the Prologue unless we are open to what is implicit, become aware of the hidden references and allusions lying below the surface, attentive to the resonances that may, to begin with, carry only the smallest of echoes, scarcely perceptible except in the subconscious. Almost every sentence of the Rule contains quotation or carries allusions to its biblical source, skilfully used by Benedict in a masterly way that suggests that he is effortlessly weaving in phrases familiar to him through his intense love of the Scriptures.[73]

It is very important to recognize this biblical underpinning and to emphasize it strongly, for unless we do we shall never appreciate how Benedict's teaching comes from careful reflection on the Word. Its purpose was simply to translate the biblical ideal into a practical way of life. The Rule, like baptism, is foundational, and we should treat it as a seminal document to be shared by all, irrespective of denomination, since it is nothing less than gospel teaching. Benedict himself would probably have been shocked to find that some of those lay people who are turning to the Rule today like to describe themselves as followers of 'Benedictine' spirituality. He has one concern only, and that is to encourage us all to become followers of the Word, of Christ, the life-giving way.

I think of the Prologue as being like the overture to some great symphony introducing us to the themes that will follow. For we are in the hands of a master. There is no doubt at all about that. From the moment that he catches our attention – as he does in that opening phrase – Benedict will not let us go. He has this vital question: 'Is there anyone here who yearns for life and desires to see good days?' (15; Psalm 34). His writing is urgent, immediate. Words pour out of him; the overriding impression is one of energy. His language, and this is as true of the verbs as of the nouns, takes us back all the time to the journey, the way, hastening, running, change. He wants people who are fully alive, who live life to the full. I am reminded of Iris Murdoch saying, at a time when she was at her most creative, 'I feel such endless vitality within me . . . A sort of vitality and joy' (I made a note of this because it gave a sense of her exuberance when she was at the height of her powers. She then went on to contrast this with 'the strangled perfection' of other novelists, and although she was speaking of writers I thought it applied more widely, and not least to many Christians.) It is something that poets write about, like Mary Oliver who in one of her best loved poems asks that ultimate question: Were we merely a visitor or did we live fully in this world? If Benedict wants to help people to turn to Christ (in the words of the baptismal formula), it is so that they might experience what he himself has so clearly found – the fullness of life that living in the presence of Christ can bring.

He is offering us the chance to live as resurrected people, and when Laurence Freeman speaks of 'the surprising energy of the Resurrection'[74] it is a reminder that new life can flow through us and so through the world. Reading the Prologue with baptism in mind makes this abundantly clear. We realize that Benedict is concerned, as is baptism, to place us in a radically new relationship with all aspects of life, above all our relationship with Christ. In the words of Patrick Barry, this is 'not a call to ascetical practices, not a programme for disciplined living'; it is 'a timeless call to inner transformation through the word of God, which can lead to the surrender of our whole being to Christ'.[75]

The whole of my being involves body, mind, spirit and not least the heart. Benedict is addressing my innermost true self, because his concern is to shape the disposition of the heart. Rather than moral or ethical directives, he forces us to think about the direction in which we are facing, our attitude and approach towards the decisions that face us in life. The essential question that the novice is asked is whether he or she is truly seeking God. It is a question for any of us: is my heart pointing in an unwavering line towards the risen Christ? Is that the direction towards which I am heading? Although Benedict will encourage me, in the end it is up to me whether I respond, and whether I take action or not.

For the Prologue is a call to action. Terrence Kardong reminds us that religion always carries the danger, which is particularly true in the case of Christianity with its huge body of subtle and complex doctrine, of becoming bogged down in a morass of speculation, or else of 'floating around as a cloud of irrelevant piety'.[76] But Benedict, just like Christ, is looking for deeds not words, as Kardong says:

'A little less talk and a little more action.' If there is a single master-theme in the Prologue, it is the need for action. The first verse states it succinctly: Accept my words and translate them into action! Throughout the exhortation, the listener is urged to take concrete steps to put the doctrine, Christian and monastic, into energetic practice.

Our response will vary, for God plays various roles in our lives at different times. He is at various times the loving father, the warrior king, an angry father, a dread lord, an eschatological judge, as we see in the opening of the Prologue. All these will ask for an obedience that is flexible and open to change. Benedict has no intention of hiding the demands of the Christian life or pretending that it will be easy or straightforward. We are being asked to undertake the commitment to a journey that we must accept will be complex, even risky. With Benedict there is no patronizing and no empty promises. Benedict, as Kardong observes, 'has no intention of hiding the difficulty of conversion and faithfulness behind the caricature of a doddering, indulgent God'.[77] But at the end of the Prologue Benedict brings us back to the paschal mystery and to the assurance of the resurrection. His final promise is that in the end we shall come through. The very last words of the Rule, in the epilogue of Chapter 73, he says:

Deo protegente, pervenies. Amen.
With God's protection you will arrive. Amen.

Lectio Divina:
A Gift for the Baptized

'The Prologue of the Rule is itself inspired by the spirit of *lectio divina* . . .' Patrick Barry gives us the key to how to approach the Prologue.[78] Here is an ancient practice within the Church, and one that is coming to play an increasingly important role for many people today in encouraging them to read prayerfully, to reflect and to gain energy from an encounter with the words of scripture.

The literal translation of *lectio divina* is spiritual reading, although prayer-filled reading gives a better idea since it suggests the kind of meditative reading that involves more than the mind and leads to prayer. 'The monastic tradition always envisions the person as a whole. It is to this whole person that the word of God is addressed.' This simple reminder comes from a member of America's largest Benedictine convent.[79] I follow it with something from the novice mistress of Stanbrook Abbey (the largest women's Benedictine community in Britain), who says that the essence of *lectio* is 'to engage with a text that is a living, life-transforming way, through the gift of the Holy Spirit; to perceive the Word in the words'.[80]

'The entire monastery – and in microcosm the heart of each monk – is nothing other than an echo chamber for the word of God . . . each monastery, each monk, each Christian becomes a house of God, *domus Dei* . . . ' Monastics have always given a central place to the Bible in their lives. It was their daily sustenance; they spoke of it as their daily bread, and they fed on it and found it life-giving. 'May the sunrise find you with the Bible in your hand!' When Evagrius says this it brings a sense of the part that the presence of scripture played in daily life, beginning at the start of the day. We have already seen how Benedict himself was saturated with scriptural quotations and allusions. The life of the monastery of his day meant the daily exposure of all its members to the Word: through the saying of the entire psalter of 150 psalms each week, biblical readings at each of the seven daily offices, in addition to scriptural canticles and antiphons. Then there was reading aloud at meals, as well as time set aside for private reading, which was increased on Sundays and in Lent.

Yet, to the surprise of many people, there is no separate chapter on *lectio* in the Rule, and nowhere does Benedict tell us how to do *lectio*. Living long before the days of method and technique for prayer there was no need to describe or dictate on such things since the whole of the monastic life was in effect an engagement with scripture and with prayer. It was the twelfth-century Carthusian monk Guido who gave it its classical formulation, imposing on it the four steps or stages with which it is now commonly associated: *lectio, meditatio, oratio, contemplatio*: reading, meditation, prayer, contemplation. It is not my intention to go into this any further here since it is very fully dealt with in any number of recent books, some of which are listed in the notes at the end of this book.[81] Taking time with the Word of God through a process of quiet repetition and assimilation will allow us to become progressively attuned to its subtle echoes in our hearts and leads us quite naturally into prayer. When we handle words gently, with reverence and respect, it is not unlike the practice of monastic hospitality – being fully attentive and open and receptive, with eyes and ears, heart and mind.

It asks for the discipline of close reading, of paying attention to every word and phrase. I am brought back once again to the reverence that Benedict is looking for in all aspects of life. In the case of *lectio* it means reading quietly and slowly, keeping ourselves silent and receptive in order that we may listen. The word ponder, derived from the Latin *pondus*, weight, always gives me the mental picture of holding a word in the palm of my hand, feeling its shape and weight, coming to delight in its presence. Inevitably the picture of Mary pondering things in her heart comes to mind. It is much like reading poetry, and like poetry it gains from being said aloud, which allows the cadences and rhythm to emerge. All this will make demands and take time, sustained attention and concentration. It means being willing to carve out time that could have been spent on other things, recognizing its importance and giving it primacy by not allowing anything else to invade that sacred space. For unless I am silent and receptive I shall not be ready to open my heart, making myself vulnerable to God's word, which like a two-edged sword pierces through to the very bone and marrow.

'This gift-task is for each of the baptised.' Sr Laurentia Johns' description brings out beautifully how it is at once both demand and gift. Its gift is to bring us into an ever-deepening relationship to the God whom we seek and to the figure of Christ who calls us. But if it is truly an enriching experience then it should become '*lectio* in action' (a phrase from Patrick Barry) and bring forth fruit in our lives. What that may be, and how it will change at different moments in life, will vary. But I am reminded once again that Benedict is looking not only for words but for deeds, and I cannot be true to my baptism unless it makes a difference to the way in which I live. We do this so that we may be drawn more closely into becoming that uniquely beloved person whom we were created to be. But we are also looking beyond ourselves to the wider Church, praying that reflective and prayerful reading may take us beyond the divisions and controversies to what we as Christians share, 'the words of scripture and the reality of our common baptism'.[82]

It is good to be reminded that reading in monasteries and convents throughout the Middle Ages would have meant reading aloud. Monastic life revolved around the word, and monks and nuns would naturally hear the Scriptures and the works of the Fathers in the hours they spent in choir and in the refectory during meals. And when it came to times of private reading on their own they would expect to enunciate the words with their lips in a low murmuring tone. The aural sense was as a result just as important as the visual perusal of the text, which, as Jean LeClerq tells us in his classic work *The Love of Learning and the Desire for God*, gave rise to 'a muscular memory of the words pronounced and an aural memory of the words heard'.

Poets know how effective it is to read aloud. T. S. Eliot says that it is one of the best things that a poet can do, and Ted Hughes told Sylvia Plath[83] that silent reading only employs part of the brain, and that means a loss both of understanding and of emotional charge. Perhaps this section of the book could bring a chance to recover this lost art, and find out if it brings a gain both to the intellect and to the emotions as Ted Hughes seems to suggest.

In the next chapter we turn to the Prologue, reading it slowly and meditatively to discover what Benedict says to us today about living our baptismal vows.

III

REFLECTIONS

Listen

'Obsculta!'

'Listen . . . listen . . . listen again.'[84] This is a powerful opening to the Prologue. The Latin word carries a sense of intent listening, the note is one of immediacy and urgency. This is 'a trumpet call',[85] a call to arouse and awaken us.

Whether I hear it as a command or an invitation it is an arresting first word, meant to make us stop in our tracks, and to pay attention. The purpose is to alert us to what is to follow, which will make a total demand on us: the fullness of listening with the whole person, and not least with the heart. One of Benedict's most memorable and significant aphorisms will come later: 'the ear of the heart'. It gives me the key as to how I should approach the Prologue and the way in which I should reflect on it, and pray with it. I remind myself that what Benedict meant by the heart is the totality of myself, the inner secret of a person, that which is deep within each of us which can probably best be described by an image such as 'the cave of the heart'.

If Benedict is going to bring me face to face with my true self it forces me to ask if I am ready for this. Am I prepared to listen from a place that is open and not closed, vulnerable and not protected? For unless this is the case all that Benedict is going to lay out before me in the Prologue will leave me untouched.

It is immediately clear that we are in the hands of an experienced teacher who, like all good teachers, will repeat his message in a slightly different form. After his opening sentence, 'Listen carefully, my son, to the master's instructions, and attend to them with the ear of your heart' (1), he will say it insistently, time and again, sometimes in his own voice, sometimes in a quotation from scripture.

'If you hear his voice today, do not harden your hearts.' (10)
'You that have ears to hear, listen . . . ' (11)
Let us listen well to what the Lord says.' (24)
'Come and listen to me.' (12)

How lovingly Benedict addresses us as he asks, 'What could be sweeter, dearest brothers, than this voice of the Lord, who invites us?'(19).[86]

Whose voice is this? The question is immaterial since whether he is speaking or whether it is 'the divine voice', the voice of the Lord, he has only one purpose, and that is to point me toward the figure of Christ himself. This then is how I must start – by my willingness to listen intently with the whole of my self.

This is exhortation, a genre common to the wisdom literature of the Bible, and it sets a tone of practical guidance and help that we need as we set out on our Christian journey as followers of Christ. Benedict will give us encouragement but he is a realist and knows that even though this is a loving call, many of us will find it difficult to respond to what might seem like dictates and demands, unless we can do so with an inner conviction.

And that is why I find that I am ready to listen to what I hear in the Prologue. Benedict is addressing 'the disposition of the heart'. He wants to shape my attitude, the way in which I approach my life. His is not a voice that threatens, but a gentle voice that wants to shape and mould through love. This is the first step and the rest will follow. There are echoes of the central prayer of the Jewish people:

Hear, O Israel . . .
What does the LORD your God require of you?
To walk in all his ways,
to love him and to keep his commandments
with all your heart and all your soul. (Deuteronomy 10.12)

If the intention of this first, and foundational, reflection is to insist on the importance of listening, of deep, intentional listening, I next need to look into the depths of my heart – since my heart is the instrument of this sort of listening – and ask myself what it is that makes it so difficult, perhaps even prevents it. For listening is no passive affair; it is conscious, willed action, it requires my whole attention, focused and controlled. I need to ask myself why I so often find it so difficult.

So now a short act of self-awareness: is it the bombardment of external sounds – or is it the continuous chattering of my thoughts? Or could it simply be that by being so over-busy I have built a barrier (perhaps one that I do not even recognize myself) so that I allow myself no time for the cultivation of that inner space of silence, that heart of stillness, which I can enter and where in quietness I might welcome the Word and, like the woman of Samaria, draw from the waters?

For I must remember that I am listening to the Word, to Christ. When I think about the voice of Christ I try to recall its various manifestations in his earthly life. I hear it sometimes encouraging and cajoling, at other times challenging and demanding. And then, since my reflections and prayers must inevitably be drawn to the paschal mystery, I think of the voice from the cross where, even at a time of almost unimaginable pain, Christ is calling for forgiveness, making excuses for those who do not realize what they are doing, speaking in what St Aelred of Rievaulx calls 'that wondrous voice, full of gentleness and love'.

We listen to Benedict because he only speaks out of what he himself knows. The foundation for his subsequent life, as the founding father of a household of brothers for whom he wrote his Rule, came out of his experience of the cave at Subiaco. Those were the years that he spent in solitude and silence, a time, in the words of St Gregory the Great, of 'holding himself still before the gaze of God'.[87] This is a wonderful description of contemplation, silence and attention – and I feel that when Benedict is telling us to listen it is because he knows that that was the way in which he came to know God, and that gave him the foundation for his own work of love in the world.[88]

Son

'Listen carefully, my son' (1)

This is the opening invitation of the Prologue and Benedict is addressing each of us as his child. We can hear the warmth in his voice. The tone so direct and intimate that it is almost as though he never quite forgets the individual who is standing in front of him and into whose eyes he is looking as he speaks with such urgency.[89] The significance of his words, however, is lost on us unless we see the depths of the image that the word 'son' carries for him through its scriptural resonances and allusions. For what he has in mind here is the parable of the prodigal son, and that is the figure with whom he wants us to identify as we set out with him on his way of life.

This is exhortation, urging us to pay attention to his message, to take action, to recognize that within each of us is the prodigal, and that we must, like him, move forward to claim life. This is the fullness of life, which Benedict himself has come to know and which he wants now for all of us. At its heart lies the relationship with a loving father, and it is only too clear that Benedict is writing out of his own experience of that, and that he wants to share with us what he has himself found.

But the very fact of being willing to listen to the Rule means that, already, by that very desire, we are already on the way, coming back to the father. This, Damasus Winzen says quite simply, 'is the key to the whole'. 'The one who is willing to listen . . . is that already, by that very desire, *filius*, he is son. He is the prodigal son, he is coming back, and he is accepted by his father.'[90]

So here Benedict plunges us at once into this parable, which is not only the story of the journey of all our lives, but also a story that we repeat time and again throughout our life. Each one of us is the prodigal. The story of the prodigal is the story of each of us. We can all identify with the prodigal, and the purpose of the Prologue, as of the waters of baptism, is to bring us back, when we have strayed, when we have squandered everything and forsaken the right road.

The generous father has heaped so many good gifts (I think both literally and figuratively) on me but I have become careless, ungrateful and unaware, squandering them, until the terrible moment of truth, when I come to myself. It is as though the fog clears in my mind and enables me to see just where I am and what I am doing to myself. By listening to the voice of God speaking to my innermost self I open my eyes to see with clarity where my own folly and selfishness have brought me.

Perhaps it is time to rewrite its title as the parable of the loving father. Baptism sets us out on the search for God but only because God is first seeking us. He stands there with arms wide open, with his offer of unconditional acceptance and love, of forgiveness, and with the new robe and the table groaning with a banquet – a celebration, just as at the conclusion of baptism, of light and colour, feasting and rejoicing!

When we think of how Rembrandt painted this we can see those dusty and bruised feet, damaged and bandaged. (They meet us at eye-level if we stand, as Henri Nouwen did so memorably, in front of the original painting in St Petersburg.[91]) It has been a long hard journey since that starting point, the moment of *metanoia*, when the prodigal comes to himself, the scales fall from his eyes, and he sees so clearly how he has squandered all the good things that the father had heaped upon him. Now instead he is envying the pigs and their husks, which is a vivid picture of how 'emptied and gutted' he must have felt, in those memorable words of Thomas Merton, as he too looked around at the end of his early years and saw how they had been wasted and had brought him nowhere. That moment of self-knowledge, of listening to the voice of his innermost depths, is the moment of revelation. It brings to the prodigal, as to me, the clarity to see exactly where I am and what I need to do – this is *metanoia*, the turning round, the repentance that is necessary in order to stir him to set out on the journey.

Rembrandt shows us the first moment of contact at the home-coming. The father who has been waiting so patiently for the son to come home has run out along the road, throwing dignity to the winds, in order to rush out and meet him. Here is an active, seeking God, reaching out to bring us home, and greeting us with the offer of the chance to begin a genuinely new relationship. Now as the son kneels before that stooping figure of the father, we see the firm grip of the hands on the shoulders. One hand seems strong, the other gentler; the balance between challenge and succour. This is a moment of stillness. It will be followed by the feasting, the new robe, the warmth and welcome of the banquet – the eucharistic table.

So too for us – the loving father, running in order to meet us halfway, not even allowing us to give the prepared penitential speech. It is not needed – we are forestalled by this offer of total acceptance and unconditional love. This moment of the welcoming reception is the promise of new life, the certainty of that forgiveness that will happen time and time again – just as our rebirth can happen time and time again.

We read this parable time and again and always find something new, for as Luther told us 'it is the Gospel within the Gospel'. If I now identify myself with the prodigal as Benedict wants me to do, I can see it as my own story, and thus make it the starting point of letting the words of the Prologue become a meditation on baptism. For baptism means the journey towards the Father who is wanting to welcome us home.

Beloved

'You are my son, the Beloved, my favour rests on you'

At the moment of baptism, the moment when the son steps up out of the Jordan, these are the words that he hears. So here is another scriptural resonance that Benedict's use of the word 'son' at the opening of the Prologue carries for us. It leads us into a further reflection on how by baptism we have become 'sons by adoption', we are loved and favoured.

So too for any of us as we rise from the water of baptism we shall hear the loving welcome:

> The voice from Heaven will say
> 'he has now become my son',
> and that belongs to those who are baptised –
> sons not by nature but by adoption . . .
> He is Son eternally,
> But you receive that grace by advancement.[92]

'There, at the waters of the Jordan, Jesus Christ knew who he was, with no agenda given – he simply knew that he was deeply loved.'[93] This is such a simple, even bald, statement in Patrick Barry's words. Can I hear it as something that is also true of me? This reflection gives me time to ask that question of myself. What does it mean to hear that I am chosen, destined, loved? That I am intimately loved from the very moment of conception?

'I have called you by name, you are mine.'

' I have written my name on the palm of your hand.'

This is the gift of beloved-ness, and it tells me that God delights in me. How then do I accept and use it as a gift of who I truly am? For a gift is not just given; it must also be recognized, claimed, received. If I accept and use the gift of who I truly am it will become a means to unlock and to liberate the person that I truly am called to be. This is my vocation, and Benedict wants us to hear the voice of the Lord:

> What could be sweeter than the voice of the Lord calling to us?
> See how in his love the Lord shows us the way of life. (19–20)

If Jesus returned to Galilee filled with the power of the Spirit, and with a sense of his identity and of his vocation, could this also be as true of me? The Prologue is a call, and that means vocation, and what Benedict is laying out are steps into that calling. A vocation is a calling which will make more and more of me. To follow Benedict, as to enter into baptism, will bring a sense of identity; I begin to discover who I am and to see the road along which I am to journey. My true self is under construction and it is the baptismal covenant that will help that forward, in a process of believing, and then continuing, persevering, seeking, serving, striving . . .[94]

Henri Nouwen tells us that becoming the Beloved is the great spiritual journey that we all have to make: 'Our whole life is a journey back to the One from whom we come and who calls us the Beloved.'[95] To be beloved simply means being accepted as who I am, and it is fundamental to my life – to be able to accept myself and accept others is so foundational that Benedict makes it the prayer of the novice entering the community. *Suscipe me.* He is using the words of the psalmist, and the Latin does not easily translate into one single word, for it carries connotations of being accepted, upheld, supported. It is a glorious prayer to pray. If I accept myself I do not have to live with the expectation that I am only of any worth when I am successful, which forces me to make endless demands on myself to achieve particular goals. It encourages me to rejoice in the person I am, and enjoy being myself. If God accepts and forgives me, and calls me beloved, as he does the prodigal, then I should not find myself acting in a way that is superior to God.

If God can forgive imperfections, flaws, failures and backslidings then should I not be able to do the same? To listen to the voice telling me that my vocation is to be, and to become, the beloved, is liberating and the way back to God is the way into freedom.

The Battle

'strong and noble weapons' (3)

Sin must be faced, for it is a turning away from God. It is failure to listen. In the garden Adam did not listen to God, choosing instead self-will, listening to his own wishes. When Benedict begins the Prologue by making listening his point of departure, so that everything else that he will show us will grow from this, he reveals an excellent grasp of the human psyche.

In the third sentence he tells us that 'the labour of obedience will bring you back', which is of course simply the next step that follows on from the act of listening. The word itself comes from the Latin *audiens*, to listen intently, which makes the connection clearer. Obedience is a process that starts with listening, but that must lead to hearing (since the two do not necessarily go together), which then demands a response that leads on to taking action. This is often easier in theory than in practice, and Benedict recognizes it in speaking of the *labour* of obedience. He contrasts it with the sloth of disobedience, using a word that carries connotations of drift and passivity, a lack of energy and of will-power. It tells us a great deal about where the roots of failure lie. 'So the sinful person settles down to a wilful existence that is progressively distanced from God.'[96] The commentary on this verse was illuminating – although I found that I wanted to substitute 'progressively estranged', since I felt that what was at stake here was the painful situation, known to many of us in human terms, of the breaking down of a relationship. It brings us back to the story of the prodigal whose life of drift carries him further and further away from the place where he really longs to be. The turning point comes when he pays attention, 'he comes to himself', and through listening to the voice inside himself (in his heart), and acting on what he hears, he is able to start the journey home. It all begins in the heart.

One of the favourite sayings of the early Fathers, which they repeated many times in a variety of ways, was very simple indeed:

> Within yourself you must wage war,
> the enemy proceeds out of your own heart.

There is no escaping the struggle. Benedict tells us to 'take up arms and fight'. At baptism I enlisted, and the cross made on my forehead is the seal of the king in whose service I now find myself. 'I serve Christ, the true King' was the watchword used by the martyr as he stood before his judge. If it still remains valid, and it can still apply in such totally different circumstances, I need to discover who is this lord and master under whom I am to serve.

Nowhere does Benedict ever speak of Jesus. In his first paragraph the role of Christ is firmly established with the words 'do battle for the true King, Christ the Lord'. The rest of the Prologue is marked by the same dynamic Christ-centredness. But the centrality of Christ means the centrality of the paschal mystery, and that is exactly where Benedict is leading us, until we reach the glorious conclusion of the Prologue: 'We shall through patience share in the suffering of Christ that we may deserve also to share in his kingdom. Amen.'

It is quite impossible to look back at the experience of baptism in the early Church without putting it into the context of those last three days of Christ's life on earth, and watching the unfolding of the events between Good Friday and Easter. We live out the paschal mystery in terms of seeing a drama being played out, which is nothing less than the struggle between death and life, darkness and light. It is an inescapable conflict, fundamental to all human experience. It is fought out in many different places, not least in the heart. This reflection is now going to take me into an area of battle which, just because it may not appear outwardly spectacular, is not the less heroic for being a hidden and interior struggle.

Benedict's language about warfare and his military metaphors can still apply, and armour and weapons still have a part to play, not least symbolically. A soldier must be on guard, keeping watch, alert and attentive, waiting for the first stirring of the enemy. 'Who am I? What sort of a watchman am I?' St Gregory asks a rhetorical question which I rather like to think of as a mantra that I can repeat to remind myself of the importance of vigilance (and for the monks the office of Vigils would recall that at the start of each day). The early catechumens were in no doubt of the wiles of Satan, and the lengths that he would go in pursuit of his prey. Translated into my own life this suggests the insidious ways in which evil thoughts insinuate themselves. Negativity, resentment and, above all, self-deception creep in unnoticed and take up residence and begin to do their destructive work.

'As soon as wrongful thoughts come into your hearts dash them against Christ.' This is advice that Benedict gives in Chapter 4, which many see as a form of the classic document linked to baptism, giving a practical list of good advice that the newly baptized could turn over ceaselessly in their memory so that they continued to choose 'the way that leads to life'.[97] The rock is of course Christ, and the image takes us back once again to the desert, to the rock struck by Moses from which the life-giving waters flowed. Wrong thoughts must be dealt with while they are still young, broken before they come to maturity. It may be an invisible battle but it does not mean that it is not dangerous. Serving under the banner of Christ brings freedom, and not least freedom from the fears, hidden insecurities, addictions and compulsions which hold us back. When we recognize this we can call out, addressing Satan: 'I fear you no longer.' The renunciation of evil begins here, and whenever I renew my baptism I have the opportunity to renounce evil once again, and to promise to continue to fight on the side of Christ whose cross I am secretly carrying on my forehead.

The Heart

'We must . . . prepare our hearts' (40)

'Today if you hear his voice do not harden your hearts.' The words that Benedict chooses here are taken from Psalm 94[95], the psalm recited at the start of each monastic day in the office of Vigils. I feel that it tells us that here was something he wanted his monks to recall daily, and I ask myself why this should be so – what was it that happened at Massah and Meribah? And how could something that happened in the desert, in the years that followed the crossing of the Red Sea, possibly hold any significance for me? Time and again in thinking about baptism I find that I am brought back to that scene at the Red Sea. It remains such a dramatic and powerful image: the symbol of a threshold, a frontier crossed, opening up into a new life of freedom, with its obvious parallels to the river Jordan, and then it becomes almost inevitably an allegory for baptism, the passing from the old life to the new. But it is important to remember that God's action does not end here. That initial threshold moment has to be followed by guidance, the learning experience that comes through the teaching of those older and wiser, those further along on the journey who are able to take events and circumstances and interpret them. It was in the desert that the people of Israel were trained by Moses, where they received from him the help that they needed if they were to break with the old and grow into new freedom.

It was at Massah that they rebelled, crying out to Moses: 'Why did you bring us up out of Egypt? To kill us, and our cattle, and our children with thirst?' (Numbers 21.5). They challenged him demanding to be told why they were there instead of where they had been before, which at least offered some sort of security. What should have been good – the crossing of a boundary, the opening up of a new frontier – seemed to have turned out badly, and something which should have led to trust and gratitude had instead brought bitterness and resentment. They grumbled and questioned as they put God to the test. They were in effect asking something that I know I have myself said many times, 'Where is God in all of this?'

The story of what happened at Massah reminds me of how easy it is to grumble at the circumstances and events of my life, and to question God's action and his purpose in bringing me to the place where I am now. The old translation of the Venite (as the psalm was known when it became part of the Anglican service of morning prayer) said 'err in their hearts', and so made it clear that it was in the heart that we went astray and lost sight of the goal. So when I next catch myself falling into the trap, which is so insidious, of complaining, 'What is going on here? Where is God in all of this?' I know that the answer lies in my own hands – the response of a heart open and receptive, trusting in the God who is journeying with me, traversing the desert, and who will remain beside me until I reach the promised land, the new life that began with the passing through the waters.

For here is a call to trust – an encouragement to persevere in the goodness and dependability of God. The author of Hebrews took these verses from Psalm 94[95] as the text for a sermon (Hebrews 3.7—4.13). It is a reminder that the hardening of the heart is the root of all other failure. Here it is spelt out: be attentive to the call of Christ, 'Hear his voice and apply it now, this very day, for tomorrow it may be too late.' Not only look but see his works, the wonders of the deliverance out of Egypt and his support since then. 'Take heed . . .' 'Hear his voice today.'

When I turn back to the first reflection I realize how essential is the opening word of the Prologue, *Listen*; it not only establishes the urgency of listening but of listening in the right way – that is, 'with the ear of the heart'. It was through that act of listening in the depths of his heart that the prodigal was able to return to the inviting God, the father offering his son unconditional love and acceptance. By straying from his heart, his true self, he had gone astray. His return to his heart resulted in his return to God.

How can a heart be pierced, punctured? What happens when I have become hard-hearted – or even half-hearted? Perhaps I have built up defensive walls, gradually, without noticing. In the Eastern spiritual tradition we are repeatedly warned of the dangers of 'the hardening of the heart'. It is described as brittleness or 'sclerosis', which brings about a deficient sensitivity. When he was asked about it the desert father Abbot Poimen knew the cure. He said that if stone is hard, water is by its very nature soft, and when water drops continually on a stone it hollows it out. 'So too God's word is delicate and mild, and whoever hears the word of God and reflects on it makes a space within his heart where it can enter.'

A hardened heart suggests the hardened earth, the unyielding soil, which is not fertile to the seed, to any form of new growth. The soil must be furrowed and ploughed, watered and tended:

The heart is something dynamic,
A source of life.
The whole garden of the person is irrigated from there.
It is the fountain of inner life . . .

These words, which come from an American Benedictine monastic, take me into one of the best images for the heart, that of the garden which we tend in order to make it fruitful, not only for ourselves but for others.

Inclina aurem cordis,
Incline the ear of your heart.
The idea is that the heart is an inner organ,
An inner room, so to speak,
In which the sound of God's word

May be received
And may gave a deep and resounding resonance.
The whole idea of the heart is so important.
The word of God is addressed to the heart
Because it is a word of love,
It is heart to heart talk.

I love that phrase in Luke's Gospel where he speaks of 'the abundance of the heart', for it gives the image of fullness, and I do not want to become half-hearted. Even though 'the acquisition of a heart is a life-long process' it is what I deeply desire, and I believe that if I desire it I shall find nurture and support in many ways: through other people, through prayer and study, through the circumstances of my life. But above all it will be in ways that I probably am unaware of and certainly do not understand – the inexhaustible mystery of God at work on me, the shaping, moulding, enlarging of a heart that will become increasingly permeable to God as my journey unfolds.

Transformation

*'Let us open our eyes to the light that comes from God,
and our ears to the voice from heaven' (9)*

If scripture is the hidden source of the Prologue then the biblical allusion that we find in these words is that of the transfiguration on Mount Tabor (Matthew 17.1–8), a theophany of light and thunder and the shining forth of Christ. It is evocative of that other mountain top, Sinai, the scene of the showing forth of the covenant of the love of God for Israel, that covenant of hope that a people would be rebuilt. So it would seem that Benedict's intention here is that we should identify ourselves with those disciples startled by the appearance of Christ and instructed by the voice from heaven.

The Latin phrase *attonitis auribus*, which is translated as 'astonished ears', carries the implication of being deafened by thunder, and, taken in parallel with *apertis oculis*, the opened eyes, brings a dramatic sense of the awe and wonder felt by the disciples – as I too should feel if I am to enter into this scene, and in my imagination bring echoes of that other mountain top as well.

To turn to the transfiguration is to turn to the image of light, and with it the movement from the darkness of sin and death into the light of Christ and the resurrection. If I want the scene of the transfiguration to become a means by which I deepen what must remain ultimately mystery, I find that my praying is helped by turning to an icon and I am grateful to be told that to gaze at an icon can lead me to look into 'deep wells of life and truth'.

The transfiguration is a scene that lends itself to visual images – and indeed I feel that it is only through images that I can fully enter into its significance. The art of the icon now becomes particularly appropriate since, because the lines of perspective being reversed move outward and the light must naturally follow this movement, everything converges on the eye. Traditional icons of the transfiguration (which have remained virtually unchanged in the Eastern Christian tradition for nearly a thousand years) show Christ, in pure white robes, standing on a rocky outcrop, placed against a dark background, with Moses and Elijah on either side and the disciples sprawled below. St Peter on the left is kneeling, supported on his left hand, raising his right hand to protect himself from the light; St John, in the centre, is turning his back to the light, crouching with his hand to his face; while St James falls backwards, protecting his eyes with his hand. They are not yet ready to see things with and in the light of God.[98]

Until their eyes are open, and their ears are unstopped, they will be blind and deaf to this call to rise to the light, which is a foretaste of the light of Easter, the light that God gives. But while these three are defending themselves from the light, Moses and Elijah shine, the light that comes from Christ reflected in their robes (and it is tempting to think of the new white robes of the newly baptized emerging from the water). What makes them radiant is the light coming from Christ. Here is 'the dwelling of the light', to borrow the haunting phrase from Job.

Peter, however, tries to cocoon himself, perhaps because he is frightened and wants to hold his fears at bay. For this is a call to transformation, to rise to the light that God offers, and we like him are being given the chance to respond to or reject this call. It will be a further step in the journey into the fullness of life that Benedict wants for us. The more I am receptive the more God gives.

I recognize once again the superb artistry of the Prologue! We are in the hands of a wise teacher who is leading us on gently and insistently from that first starting point, in telling us to listen, to be attentive with eye, ear, heart.

The whole process of being awake
to the presence of God in the Word
is one of transformation,
being transfigured into the likeness of Christ.[99]

The word 'transformation' carries connotations of being transformed from within, which can only happen if, and when, I am
ready and consenting to be changed. It brings to mind one of the
favourite examples used in teaching the catechumens: clay in the
hands of the potter, to be softened and moulded in the waters of
baptism. So this is the question that I must now address. Can I allow
myself to be transformed into the true self, the resurrected self? If I
see this mountain-top moment as 'the single most important
staging-post on the way'[100] of Christ's earthly journey until the
apparent dead-end of the crucifixion, can I see it as a pledge that the
way does not end there in betrayal and death? Can I allow this to
become the reassurance to bring that mountain-top experience
down to the plain?

Light

Once again the Prologue will illuminate one of the central themes of baptism, which from the earliest times was spoken of as 'enlightenment'. Benedict is now bringing us the theology of light. There are echoes of Johannine theology here, as also of Eastern mysticism, where the idea of drawing near to the Lord and being illumined is common. Contemplation of the divine light, enlightenment by the heavenly light – this is something that can be better experienced than expressed.

For while Benedict is a most practical of guides, down to earth, addressing me as worker and looking for deeds, there is also a mystical dimension to the Prologue, and if Benedict is to be an exemplar I must never forget this. There are two sides to this man, just as I must have both sides in my own life.

I shall never fully become his disciple unless I allow him to open up for me the contemplative and the mystical. Again I am ready to accept what he says because it is clear that he is only speaking of what he himself knows. At the end of his life there was that amazing scene, described by St Gregory, of him being lifted far above the world by an 'inner light', and seeing the whole world gathered into one single ray of light. It was not that the earth shrank in size – it was that his vision, his gaze, had expanded. What we see here is the mind unfolding, the heart enlarging. Benedict is seeing the world from God's viewpoint, because he himself is so absorbed in God that he sees everything in relation to God's greatness.

'The light that comes from God "the divine light".' These words stand at the head of this reflection. This is the translation of RB80 and most texts, but when we take the original Latin *deificum lumen* we will find that it lends itself to another reading. If it is translated as 'the light that makes us like God', or 'shapes us into the likeness of God', then it becomes much more profound.[101] For when we pick up the biblical references that were probably in Benedict's mind we find an echo of St Paul in 2 Corinthians 3.18: 'We all, with unveiled face, beholding the glory of the Lord, are being changed into his likeness from one degree of glory to another.'

And then St Paul develops this theme, which is of course the theme *par excellence* of the whole Prologue, and one which Benedict will bring to a glorious conclusion when he speaks of our sharing in the passion of Christ so that we may also share in his glory:

It is the God who said, "Let light shine out of darkness," who has shone in our hearts to give the light of the knowledge of the glory of God in the face of Christ. (2 Corinthians 4.6)

The mountain top we have seen to be the place of light, the place of transformation. Shall I try to close myself to this powerful light? Or shall I be open to the mystical and enter into the mysterious working of the Holy Spirit, and make this part of my baptismal vocation?

Run while you have the light of life,
lest the darkness of death overtake you. (13)

Here Benedict in typical fashion takes the words from John (John 12.35) and makes them even more dramatic by changing the original word walk into *run*. With his sense of urgency he is telling us there must be no hesitation and no delay. I cannot postpone this for, as baptism tells so vividly, we must turn towards the light. Or in the words of Psalm 33[34] (used in the baptismal preparation and so very apposite for us), 'Look towards him, and be radiant.'

'And now the eyes of the Lord will be upon me, I will be under his eye.' I think once more of the gaze of God as Benedict experienced it in the cave at Subiaco and then of the gaze which he brought to bear on the world at the end of his life.

I have found a guide who will lead me far beyond word or image – and if this reflection has brought me to silence then I am sure that that is right, and that is where I should be.

Good Deeds

'the Lord waits for us daily to translate into action, as we should, his holy teachings' (35)

'Hear – and act! Listen, hear, respond, take action . . . Benedict's words are an exhortation meant to rouse us up, and stir us into action: "Every time you begin a good work, you must pray to him most earnestly to bring it to perfection"' (4)

'We will never arrive unless we run there by doing good deeds' (22)

The Prologue belongs to the genre of wisdom literature whose purpose is to give practical wisdom, which, like any other practical art, needs to be practised. Just because it is such a splendid piece of writing, tender and lyrical, it is important to remember that it is also a hard document that yields its meaning 'not to readers but to *keepers*'. Benedict wants us to hear the call to follow Christ, and to respond by taking practical action. It is quite clear that he is writing of what he himself has experienced. His own knowledge of Christ has been for him fulfilling and life-giving and he wants the same for us. But because he has followed this path himself he has no illusions about it: he knows that it demands strenuous action. 'Human effort alone cannot do it. We need God's support and relying on that do not try to run away . . .' The tone of voice is strong, and Benedict chooses words that a philosopher would call performative, their intention being to encourage energy and action.[102]

We recognize at once just how dynamic this man is. It is interesting to discover that, when we take this much over-used word back to its original root, it carries the meaning of 'the interplay of forces'. *Dynamis* means force; the initial dynamism comes from God, and the play of forces develops when we respond to that. The Lord is seeking us! The opening of the Prologue shows us that Benedict wants to help us to establish a relationship with God, and to the succession of images that he presents – that of father and son, master and pupil – he now adds another category, that of worker. The Lord is seeking his worker.

With the context of the parable of the vineyard workers in mind, we see God inviting us to collaborate with his work, calling us to come forward, wanting us to become co-workers with him. Good intentions must lead us into 'the performance of good works' (21) The Prologue is about practical Christianity. Benedict, after all, established this in the opening sentence: welcome the advice and faithfully put it into practice. It will continue to be his underlying theme. It will occur again with the psalm-commentary on psalms 15 and 34 that he uses, as did baptismal catechetical teaching, for its purpose is a thoroughly practical one: we must translate good intention into action.

If I see baptism as a rite of initiation which marks the start of my commitment to Christ this will have to be worked out with long-term and dogged perseverance. That commitment has to be renewed, not only in my public declaration of intent, but privately and unseen in daily life. For it is there that it is going to be tested. Made with voice and mind and will, it must then be worked out, so that it is also visibly expressed.

Benedict gives many warnings about the pitfalls; he knows there are many ways of escape into self-deception that I need to guard against. That is why I need this time to prepare for the deliberate and conscious renewal of my baptismal promises. I want to make them the opportunity for making once again a conscious commitment to placing Christ at the centre of my whole life and my whole self – the spiritual, the intellectual and not least the physical, the manual, the work of my body.

I love the image of the Rule as taking us by the hand and leading us to Christ, for that brings the assumption of active co-operation, the willingness on my part to be actively engaged. At baptism I put my hand to the plough, and I must not turn back. This means perseverance, hanging on; it is linked to patience, to *patientia*, and so the passion and the paschal mystery that underlies everything in the Prologue as, God willing, it will underlie all that my Christian vocation is asking of me.

Love

Surely this must be one of the most incomparable phrases of all time. Towards the end of the Prologue Benedict gives us some of the most lyrical of his writing. These are words of such beauty that I find myself repeating them time and again, rejoicing in them, praying with them as *lectio*. In the original Latin we can see that Benedict has chosen a deliberate alliteration; sounds that get lost in English: *dilatato . . . dilectionis dulcedine*. The various ways in which the phrase can be translated gives us a sense of the riches that the words carry.

'Our hearts overflowing with the inexpressible delight of love.'

'Our hearts will warm . . . with a love full of delight.'

'Our hearts will swell with the unspeakable sweetness of love.'[103]

This image of the heart expanding through growth in the love of Christ is one of the most beautiful in the Prologue. Just a moment earlier Benedict has spoken of a love fire-tested by discipline: 'a little discipline in order to safeguard love'.[104] But now he quickly fills out the picture and shows us a love that is pure delight. It is the love of Christ, and the power of that love, that brings such a ringing conviction to what Benedict is writing here– everything has been leading up to this. Patrick Barry says that we 'can tell what this power of love meant to Benedict when he writes "We can see with what loving concern the Lord points out to us the path of life.'" The words of this reflection come into the context of that path – one of the most favourite and familiar themes. 'You will teach me the path of life,' says the psalmist in psalm 15[16], one commonly used in baptismal teaching, and one which Benedict also uses in the Prologue. And here and now we are shown the essential context in which we are to travel along that path:

> As we progress in this way of life and in faith,
> We shall run on the path of God's commandments,
> Our hearts overflowing
> With the inexpressible delight of love.

The path is nothing without love. We are here shown the keystone, as it were, on which everything else hinges: the love of Christ. As the Prologue draws towards its conclusion we realize just how totally Christ-centred is the life that Benedict is showing us. Everything points to Christ. Christ's presence is there to encourage the growth from the old self-centred person into the Christ-centred person whom he is calling us to become.

The figure of Christ has appeared at the start, in the third verse of the Prologue, and it will appear again in the penultimate verse of the final chapter, where Benedict asks us if we are hastening towards our heavenly home, and promises that with Christ's help we shall arrive (73.8). For Christ is the alpha and omega of the entire Rule, the frame of the whole, just as he is also of my life. It is only with the assistance of Christ that I can hope to keep to the way of life on which I have embarked in living out my baptismal commitment.

'The process of Christ' is a telling phrase that comes from the eighteenth-century figure William Law. It carries for me the suggestion of change and deepening, and to use it as *lectio* at this point might allow me to discover more of Christ at work in my life – and thus to find myself drawn more deeply into the mystery of who I am, the Beloved. For in the end, my purpose in following my baptismal covenant is simply this – a deepening of my relationship with Christ, so that the more I come to know him and to love him, the more I hope that I may become like him.

Everything must lead to this.
It is always the love of Christ
which is the centre of our growth process.
The focal point of all growth is growth in the love of Christ.

In choosing this image of the heart expanding, swelling, with love of Christ Benedict is telling us that throughout our lives we shall continue to learn Christ. But it will not be any abstract knowledge, rather it will be through the heart. 'Return to the heart,' I tell myself, trying to repeat it constantly, reminding myself that it is here that I enter into that relationship which puts the love of Christ at the centre of everything else.

The Paschal Mystery

'We shall through patience share in the sufferings of Christ that we may deserve also to share in his kingdom. Amen' (50)

And now as Benedict brings me to the end of the Prologue, he is drawing me into the paschal mystery. The whole rite of baptism has been a mysterious reliving of the cross and the entry into the darkness of the tomb before the rising to the new life of Easter. Here is the promise of baptism – that we who have shared through patience in the suffering of Christ will enter into a joyous share in his kingdom. This message brings the Prologue to its resounding conclusion. The Christ-life which Benedict has been showing us, and which he wants for all of us, is life in the risen Christ. What we have been learning from him is resurrection theology.

Patientia is one of the greatest virtues for Benedict and he comes back to it here as he is drawing everything together. It means waiting, endurance, lifelong perseverance. The first time it appears in the Prologue is verse 37, in the context of God's patient waiting for us to turn to him. Later on, when he comes to write his marvellous chapter on love, Benedict will use it to tell us how we are to support with the greatest patience the physical and moral defects of one another. These two examples tell us so much about the right sort of waiting and endurance. This is not about being stoical or becoming a martyr. It is something much more hidden and more mysterious: God's patience in waiting for me may well go unnoticed over a long period of time. The patience that God is looking for from any of us may be unspectacular, but nonetheless it asks of us that we hold on, do not give up. I think of how often the psalms speak of steadfastness. If I see patience as closely allied to the vow of stability I am helped to see how positive it should be, connected to joy and hope. And then when I turn my mind to the example of Christ in the garden of Gethsemani I see the ultimate example of *patientia*, suffering in obedience to doing the will of the Father – which is the prelude to the triumph of Easter.

I have been baptized into Christ. To follow Christ is to be transformed into his likeness. Benedict has this one purpose in mind: to teach us Christ, to draw us towards Christ. As I look back over the Prologue I realize how many roles Christ will play in my journey, and the different images that Benedict gives me (whether simultaneously or successively): Christ as master and teacher, Christ as the rock on whom I build, and against whom I dash my evil thoughts; Christ as the true king under whom I serve . . . In the main body of the Rule, as he develops his teachings, Benedict will use many more images: father, healer, shepherd, servant, wise physician, judge . . . But above all it is in the Prologue that he is showing me the risen Christ. This is the paschal Christ, who has come through the cross, the descent into the underworld, the rising from the grave. By this he has overcome the darkness, and brings to us who have chosen to be his friends and followers freedom from the powers of darkness, the dark forces whether they be within or without.

We can now see where Benedict has been leading us, building up to this from the start when he told us to listen and obey with willing freedom. In doing this we are following Christ, identifying with him as we watch him in his earthly life. Our union with Christ – which is of course the baptismal gift through which we are given a share in his life – has brought us to this point. What a strange and astonishing situation! Perhaps we need to be jolted, startled into exclaiming our amazement out loud as those early catechumens might have done. Can we hear these words, as though we were there in person standing with those newly baptized? They have come through the time of testing, of instruction, of waiting, and at the conclusion of the moving drama of the rite itself they stand on the threshold of their new life.

There is a danger that familiarity has blunted our own amazement. There have been so many occasions, so many homilies and explanations, words spoken and written that perhaps silence in the face of such mystery is the only possible response. And yet if we now listen to this exultant outpouring of Melito of Sardis it will take us back to the earliest days of the Church, and remind us of the living tradition of which we are a part. It is the voice of Christ whom we hear, the risen Christ as he greets us:

> I am the Christ.
> It is I who destroyed death,
> who triumphed over the enemy,
> who trampled Hades underfoot,
> who bound the strong one
> and snatched man away to the heights of heaven;
> I am the Christ.
>
> Come then . . .
> It is I who am your ransom, your life,
> your resurrection,
> your light,
> your salvation, your king.
> I am bringing you to the heights of heaven,
> I will show you the Father who is from all eternity,
> I will raise you up with my right hand.[105]

Continuing to Learn

'Therefore we intend to establish a school for the Lord's service' (45)

The Prologue opened with Benedict challenging us to listen to him, and it will end, in the final paragraph, with Benedict continuing to play his role as the encouraging master inviting us to persevere in Christ's teaching until death. The words of Matthew 11.29 may have been running through his mind: 'Learn from me; for I am gentle and lowly in heart ...'

As he draws towards the end of the Prologue Benedict becomes emphatic in speaking of the importance of continuing in the teachings of Christ. The significance that it holds for him is shown in the fact that he mentions it in different forms no less than three times in his final paragraph. He begins by saying that he wants to establish a school for the Lord's service (45); he then speaks of running on the path of God's commandments (*via mandatorum Dei*) (49), until in the final verse he brings everything to a triumphant conclusion: 'never swerving from his instructions, then, but faithfully observing his teaching ...' (*magisterio ... doctrinam*) (50)

In Chapter 73, his final chapter, Benedict says that his Rule was written 'for beginners'. He is of course showing humility, but he is also making a vitally important point for his disciples. He is reminding us not to be content with this brief and modest rule; it sets out the minimal demands but we cannot stop here. Like the people of the Exodus, after crossing the Red Sea there is still a long journey ahead to the promised land. Having come to the Jordan the same is true for us as baptized Christians. Baptism is a point of departure and as we continue to make our way to our heavenly home, we shall need further training, instruction, inspiration. The account of baptism in the first part of this book showed the seriousness with which candidates underwent preparation, and their instruction did not stop with the actual rite of baptism. If I am to follow the example of Benedict's disciples and of the early catechumens, it is clear that I must continue on the path of learning.

How am I to keep alive my baptismal commitment? How am I to avoid mental sloth and inertia, the drift that Benedict has so vividly warned me against? What should I be doing in order to refresh and deepen my faith and practice? When I turn to the Prologue I see that in the areas of both practical help and spiritual encouragement I have been given very substantial teaching. When I read the baptismal homilies of Cyril or Chrysostom or Theodore I find inspiration, vivid language, splendid oratory, material that, like the Rule, will draw me back time and again to discover further riches.

This is wisdom, not narrowly cerebral, or only concerned with the intellect. I cannot hope to live out my baptismal promises if I do no more than recite the creed in church as a public statement of belief. Benedict has told us to prepare 'our hearts and bodies' (40). He is always addressing the totality of the self – myself as a person made up of mind, body, spirit. Each element has its role in the balanced life, and I must treat each with due reverence and respect so that they grow and develop appropriately:

Attention to the art of prayer, both personal and shared, so that I may be taken further into areas that I may not yet have explored.

Attention to the physical self, to acknowledging the part played by my body's strengths and weaknesses; listening to the senses and being sensitive to the understanding that they can bring.

Attention to the imagination, increasing awareness of the importance of the visual, taking pleasure in poetry, discovering the power latent in symbol and image, and in particular reading the Scriptures time and again as though for the first time. Above all I feel that I should undertake the sort of study or serious reading that will make demands on the mind and prevent it from growing slack and superficial.

Benedict is clear about the importance of reading widely and intelligently. While the Bible must of course remain the foundation of any Christian life, there are in addition treasures both new and old. He tells his disciples to read from divergent sources, just as he himself has been influenced by the different monastic traditions with which he is clearly familiar. He cites John Cassian and the desert fathers, St Basil whom the monks of the Eastern Church have always considered their greatest ancestor. He describes their writings as tools, and those who fail to make use of them are castigated as lazy, negligent, unobservant. That last word is one which brings me back to what I have been told so many times by Benedict – the importance of being attentive, alert, aware.

One way of making my reading come alive is to cultivate an inner dialogue by which I question and discuss the text in front of me. Benedict gives us many examples of a relationship of this sort: the teacher, the master, the father addressing the pupil, the disciple, the son. This makes for interaction between two voices, something reciprocal, the giving and receiving which will encourage ideas to grow and to change, and thus I hope become a source of fresh energy. So I am brought back once more to Benedict's concern to point us towards whatever will be challenging and life-enhancing on our journey to God.

IV

ANTHOLOGY

Anthology

Introduction

The first word of the Prologue is 'listen', that simple, resounding word whose significance we should never underestimate. This book concludes with material set out in order that we may listen to it with the ear of the heart, take time with it, allow it to lead us into prayerful reflection – and then hope that it may make a difference in the way we live our lives. The intention of preparing ourselves for the renewal of our baptismal commitment has taken us not only into the area of the verbal – for the recitation of the articles of belief of the creed remain at the heart of baptism – but also into image and symbol, words as song and poetry, words used for storytelling and remembering. This was part of the riches of baptismal catechetal teaching and it has been a theme throughout this book. For baptism deals with what is timeless and inescapable in human experience; it speaks with a voice common to artists, poets and philosophers of what is primordial in all human experience: death and life, darkness and light, the life-giving and the life-denying.

This light–dark symbolism will recur throughout the Bible, as it does also in the myths and traditions of peoples worldwide who feared the forces of darkness, as many still do in more primal parts of the world. Perhaps it is a fear that lies closer to many of us than we dare to admit.

Perhaps we do not sufficiently often think of baptism as new birth, carrying something of the mystery of the birth of a child, or the mystery of the coming into being of the universe. The Bible opens with words about the genesis of heaven and earth that are not words of information but words of a song about how the world came into being. The first chapter of Genesis opens up a primordial scene: darkness and light are presented as cosmic qualities of the first day where we read how the darkness which was upon the face of the deep was dispelled by the breath of God brooding over the water and how the breathing condensed into the creative Word and light shone forth. God is not described or announced – he is presented to us through his creative activity in dismissing darkness. We are plunged at once into the equilibrium, the cyclical rhythm, of light and dark, day and night.

> Looking westward across the darkening sea the people of Palestine could see the nightly death of the sun – sometimes in the redness of fire or blood: in the morning, having passed through the dark waters of night, the sun was born anew in the glory of light.[106]

That light–darkness symbolism will be a recurrent theme of the passages that follow. God at work in history, and at work in our own individual lives, is something to be told time and time again. I hope that reading these actual words will help to remind us that we are the heirs of a long story, heard by countless generations down the ages. It is a story which does not tire for, as I have tried to show, its symbolism is archetypal and it touches our own life-experience. And so we listen to the voices of these early fathers, hearing yet again the beginning in the garden of Eden, the drama of the crossing of the Red Sea, the Exodus, and the years of wandering in the desert until we come to the events of Christ's earthly life and watch the unfolding of the crucifixion until finally we are brought to the glory of the resurrection.

And how we see that the way in which Benedict addressed us at the opening of the Prologue, as both the beloved and the prodigal, is one that may help to deepen the way in which to approach these readings. For to prepare for the renewal of our baptismal promises is a reminder that our lives repeat that journey time and time again in a pattern of transformation, of the old being made over into the new, that will continue until the day of our death – until finally the paschal mystery will at last become a reality.

Above all, these passages are not meant for the purely cerebral approach. These writings remind us that it is impossible to separate the spiritual and the material. Christ the incarnate son of God welcomes us into the mystery of the incarnation, and baptism itself reminds us that we are body-persons. To kneel, turn and rise is a physical act; the body will be stripped and rubbed with oil, plunged naked into the water before it is reclothed and finally fed. The naked self is at the heart of baptism. And the frequent comparison with the clay in the hands of the potter is a vivid image to remind us of how material can be shaped and moulded in the hands of the maker.

This is what baptism re-enacts, and we have seen that it not only engages with the five senses, but that it also involves the four elements – earth, air, fire and water (which ancient Greeks saw as the building blocks of the world). Baptism makes our earthliness inescapably present and reminds us of our physicality. We see ourselves as clay, earthly matter, being plunged into the waters to be shaped. We see the role of the Holy Spirit. The lamps which signal the ceremony are the source of flame and light. It is as though the whole of creation is here brought into play, and something that is foundational to all human existence is being taken up and becomes the threshold into the new life in the risen Christ.

Above all, to recall our baptism brings us the opportunity to give thanks for what John Chrysostom called 'the indescribable goodness of the love God shows to the human race'. The anthology therefore starts with the theme of gratitude for this gift that we have received at the hand of a generous and loving Father.

The extracts that follow are taken from instructions to catechumens and baptismal homilies. The headings are mine, chosen in order to make the material more accessible and usable. My hope is that the reading of these original texts will bring a sense of the expectation which surrounded preparation for baptism, and the sense of the immediacy and the urgency of just how momentous and life-changing an event it would be.

I have taken the material from three main sources.

- St Cyril of Jerusalem was born of Christian parents in 315, and became the bishop of Jerusalem in 348. His *Catecheses* were delivered as a Lent course in Jerusalem in about 350. He died in 386.
- St John Chrysostom was born *c.* 347 in Antioch (just a year or two before Cyril gave his lectures). He was baptized in 370, ordained priest, and elevated in 397 to the patriarchate of Constantinople – an unhappy move, for, a deeply spiritual man, he lacked worldly wisdom, made enemies, was deposed in 403, exiled in 404, and died on 14 September 407.
- Theodore of Mopsuestia was born in Antioch *c.* 350, and served as a priest there until 392 when he became bishop of Mopsuestia, a town about 100 miles away, where he remained until his death in 428. It was probably during his time at Antioch that he preached the 16 catechetical sermons.

A GRATEFUL HEART

The wonderful, unbelievable thing is that every difference and distinction of rank is missing here. If anyone happens to be in a position of worldly importance or conspicuous wealth, if he boasts of his birth or the glory of this present life, he stands on just the same footing as the beggar in rags, the blind man or the lame. Nor does he complain at this since he knows that all such differences have been set aside in the life of the spirit; a grateful heart is the only requirement.

John Chrysostom

THE GENEROSITY OF GOD

Consider, my beloved, the abundance of God's goodness from the beginning. For if, without your having worked for it nor shown any qualification, he thinks you worthy of such a gift and pardons all the sins you have committed in your life, what return are you likely to merit from a loving God if after such great kindness you learn to be grateful and determine to make a contribution of your own? . . .

In human affairs nothing similar has ever been seen . . . But in the service of our Master . . . even before we begin our efforts and offer anything of our own, he forestalls us and shows his own generosity, so that his many kindnesses may induce us to take thought for our own salvation . . .

God considered that one who was heedless of such blessings [i.e. the Garden of Eden] was worthy once more of his great kindness. So if you try to be grateful for these indescribable gifts that are being granted to you, and if you are vigilant to preserve them once they are granted, who can say what kindness you will win from him, if you succeed in preserving them? He it was who said 'To everyone who has will more be given, and he will have abundance'. One who makes himself worthy of what he has already received deserves to enjoy greater blessings still.

John Chrysostom

Approach with care

Let the heavens be glad, and let the earth rejoice, because of those who are about to be sprinkled with hyssop and cleansed with spiritual hyssop, that is, with the power of Christ, who in his passion was offered drink on a stalk of hyssop. Let the powers of heaven rejoice, and let those souls who are to be united with their spiritual bridegroom prepare themselves. For a voice cries in the wilderness: 'Prepare the way of the Lord'.

So, then, children of justice, listen to John's appeal: 'Make straight the way of the Lord'. Clear away all that impedes you, all obstacles, that you may go straight towards eternal life. Purify your souls with a sincere faith and prepare them to receive the Holy Spirit. Begin to wash your garments through repentance . . . God forbid that any of those who have been enrolled [i.e. the catechumens] should hear him say: 'Friend, how did you get here without a wedding garment?' May you all rather hear the words: 'Well done, good and faithful servant' . . .

Until now you have been standing outside the door. It is my prayer for you that soon you will be able to say: 'The king has brought me into his innermost room.'

Brethren, this is a matter of great importance, and you must approach it with care. Each of you will stand in the presence of God, before countless hosts of angels. The Holy Spirit will set a seal upon your souls, and you will be enlisted into the service of the great King.

Cyril

Telling the story: God at work in history

The Garden of Eden

From the very beginning God has never ceased to bless the human race. For as soon as he created the first man, at once he put him to dwell in the garden of Paradise and gave him a life of ease, allowing him the freedom of all that was in the garden except for a single tree. But once the man had intemperately allowed himself to be deceived by the woman, he rode roughshod over the command that was given to him and abused the great honour that had been paid him.

Here too you see the extent of God's love for man. It would have been just if one who had been so ungrateful for the benefits prepared for him had been judged unworthy of any further pardon and set outside God's providence. Not only did God not do this, but he was like a loving Father with an undisciplined son. In his instinctive love for the boy, he does not measure punishment by the fault; nor does he completely let him go free, but chastises him with moderation so as not to drive him to greater evil and the shipwreck of his life . . .

It is almost as if God had said to him: 'This ample ease and freedom which you enjoyed has led you to this act of grave disobedience and has made you forget my commandments. Consequently I am condemning you to toil and hardship, so that by working the land you may have a continual reminder of your own disobedience . . . I order you to go back to the dust from which you have been taken. "You are dust and to dust you shall return".'

To increase his sorrow and make him perceive his own fall, God made him dwell not far from Paradise and walled off his entry into it, so that the continual sight of what he had forfeited in his heedlessness might serve as a perpetual warning and make him in future more careful to keep the commands that were given to him.

But even so, God in his love did not abandon the human race. He showed the devil the futility of his attempts and showed man the extent of the care he has for him – through death he gave him immortality. Just think. The devil threw man out of Paradise; the Master brought him into heaven. The profit is greater than the loss.

John Chrysostom

MOSES AND CHRIST

Now turn your mind from past to present, from symbol to reality. Of old Moses was sent into Egypt by God, but in our era Christ is sent into the world by the Father. As Moses was appointed to lead his afflicted people from Egypt, so Christ came to deliver the people of the world who were overcome by sin. The tyrant of old pursued the ancient Jewish people as far as the sea, and here and now the devil, bold and shameless, the source of all evil, followed you up to the waters of salvation. Pharaoh was submerged in the sea, and the devil disappears in the waters of salvation.

Cyril

The Exodus

The Jews saw miracles. You will see greater and more glorious miracles than those which accompanied the exodus of the Jews from Egypt. You did not see the Pharaoh and his troops drowning; but you saw the devil and his armies overwhelmed by flood waters. The Jews passed through the sea; you have passed through death. They were snatched from the grasp of the Egyptians; you from the grip of demons. The Jews cast off a foreign yoke; you the much more galling slavery of sin.

Shall I tell you of another way which has brought you a greater honour than ever they had? Though Moses was their fellow slave and kinsman, the Jews could not bear to look upon his glorified face. But you have seen the face of Christ in his glory. These are the triumphant words of Paul, 'And we all with unveiled faces reflect the glory of the Lord'.

At that time the Jews had Christ to follow them, but in a much truer sense Christ now follows us. Then the Lord walked at their side for the grace of Moses; now the Lord walks at your side not only because of the grace of Moses, but also because of your obedience. Once Egypt had been left behind, the desert awaited them; when your journey is over, heaven awaits you. Their guide, that famous leader, was Moses; our guide and famous leader is another Moses, God himself.

Moses would raise his hands to heaven and call down from there manna, that is the bread of angels. But our Moses now raises his hand to heaven, and brings us food that lasts for ever. Moses struck the rock and released streams of water; our Moses lays his hand upon the table, he strikes the spiritual board and draws forth the fountains of the Spirit. In its centre there is as it were, a fountain, so that the flocks come there from afar and wide and are refreshed with its saving waters.

Such is the fountain that we have, this the well-spring of life, this the banquet table abounding with good things past numbering, which makes us strong with spiritual gifts.

John Chrysostom

The scene at the Jordan

Jesus sanctified baptism when he himself was baptised . . . He was baptised in order that he might impart grace and dignity to those who receive the sacraments.

He bathed in the river Jordan and, after imparting the fragrance of his godhead to the waters, came up from them. Him the Holy Spirit visited in essential presence, like resting upon like. Similarly with you . . .

Cyril

The cross

The Gospel relates Christ had died and was still hanging on the cross, the soldier approached him and pierced his side with the spear, and at once there came out water and blood. The one was a symbol of baptism, the other of the mysteries [i.e. the eucharist]. The soldier, then, pierced his side: he breached the wall of the holy temple, and I found the treasure and acquired the wealth. Similarly with the lamb. The Jews slaughtered it in sacrifice, and I gathered the fruit of that sacrifice – salvation.

'There came out from his side water and blood.' Dearly beloved, do not pass the secret of this great mystery by without reflection.

For I have another secret mystical interpretation to give. I said that baptism and the mysteries were symbolised in that blood and water. It is from these two that the holy Church has been born 'by the washing of regeneration and the renewal of the Holy Spirit', by baptism and by the mysteries. Now the symbols of baptism and the mysteries come from his side.

John Chrysostom

'A TIME TO DIE AND A TIME TO BE BORN'

You were conducted by the hand to the holy pool of sacred baptism, just as Christ was conveyed from the cross to the sepulchre close at hand.

You submerged yourselves three times in the water and emerged; by this symbolic action you were secretly re-enacting the burial of Christ three days in the tomb. Just as our Saviour spent three days and nights in the womb of the earth, so you upon first emerging were representing Christ's first day in the earth, and by your immersion his first night. For at night one can no longer see but during the day one has light; so you saw nothing when immersed as if it were night, but you emerged as if to the light of day. In one and the same action you died and were born: the water of salvation became both tomb and mother for you.

What Solomon said in another context is apposite to you: 'There is a time to be born, and a time to die', but the opposite is true in your case – there is a time to die and a time to be born. A single moment achieves both ends, and your begetting was simultaneous with your death.

What a strange and astonishing situation! We did not really die, we were not really buried, we did not really hang from a cross and rise again. Our imitation was symbolic, but our salvation is real.

Christ truly hung from a cross, was truly buried, and truly rose again. All this he did gratuitously.

Cyril

BEFORE THE CROSS

Tomorrow, on Friday at the ninth hour, you must have certain questions asked of you and you must present your contracts to the Master. Nor do I make mention to you of that day and that hour without some purpose. A mystical lesson can be learned from them. For on Friday at the ninth hour the thief entered paradise; the darkness, which lasted from the sixth to the ninth hour, was dissolved, and the Light, perceived by body and mind, was taken as a sacrifice for the whole world. For at that hour Christ said: 'Father, into thy hands I commend my spirit.' Then the sun we see looked on the Sun of Justice shining from the cross and turned back its own rays.

Therefore, when you are about to be led [into the church] at the ninth hour, do you also recall to mind the great number of virtuous deeds and count those gifts which await you; you will no longer be on earth, but your soul will raise itself up and lay hold of heaven itself.

John Chrysostom

The Renunciation of Evil

THE CONTRACT TO RENOUNCE EVIL

The priest then instructs you to say, *I renounce you, Satan, your pomp, your worship and your works.* There is great power in these few words. For the angels who are present, and the invisible powers rejoice at your conversion and, receiving the words from your lips, carry them to the common master of all things, where they are inscribed in the books of heaven.

Have you seen the terms of the contract? After the renunciation of the Evil One and all the works he delights in, the priest instructs you to speak again as follows: *And I pledge myself, Christ, to you.* Do you see the overwhelming goodness of God? From you he receives only words, yet he entrusts to you realities, a great treasure. He forgets your past ingratitude; he remembers nothing of your past; he is content with these few words.

John Chrysostom

'I RECOGNISE MY SAVIOUR'

When you say 'I renounce Satan' you mean: Now we have nothing in common with him. I have hardly realised the evils in which he tried to involve us every day; hardly understood the extent of the harm suffered by Adam, the father of us all, when he listened to the devil, the extent of the ills he incurred, together with those who freely submitted themselves to the devil and down the years chose to become his slaves. But now that a great and marvellous grace has appeared through Christ himself, a grace that has freed us from the Tyrant's oppression, liberated us from this slavery, won for us good things in wonderful abundance – now I know my benefactor, I recognise my Saviour. For truly my benefactor is my Saviour, who created me when I was not, who grants me favours every day, who does not turn away from me even when I rebel . . . Once for all I renounce Satan, I avoid his company and pledge myself by vow never to seek it again. I shall have nothing to do with him, I shall avoid him like a dangerous enemy, for he was the cause of evils without number . . . This is the meaning of 'I renounce'.

Theodore

IN THE HANDS OF THE POTTER

The water you enter is like a crucible in which you are reshaped to a higher nature: you lay aside your old mortality and assume a nature that is completely immortal and incorruptible. You are born in water because you were formed originally from earth and water, and when you fell into sin the sentence of death made you totally corruptible. The potters are also in the habit, when vessels which they fashion are damaged, to refashion them again with water so that they may be remade and reconstructed and so it recovers its true form. This is the reason why God ordered the prophet Jeremiah to go to the potter; and he went and saw him working on a vessel which, because it was marred, he cast in the water, remade, and brought to its former state, and then God said to him: 'O house of Israel, can I not do with you as this potter has done?' Because we too were formed from earth and clay – 'You too were formed from a piece of clay, like me' (Job 33.6) . . .

As an earthen vessel, which is being remade and refashioned in water, will remain in its softer nature and be clay as long as it has not come in contact with fire, but when it has been thrown on fire and baked on it, it will undoubtedly be remade and refashioned, so also we, who are in a mortal nature, rightly receive the grace of the Holy Spirit, which hardens us more than any fire can do.

Theodore

The smelting furnace

This bath does not merely cleanse the vessel but melts the whole thing down again. Even if a vessel has been wiped off and carefully cleansed, it still has the marks of what it is and still bears the traces of the stain. But when it is thrown into the smelting furnace and is renewed by the flames, it puts aside all the dross and when it comes from the furnace, it gives forth the same sheen as newly moulded vessels. When a man takes and melts down a gold statue which has become filthy with the filth of years and smoke and dirt and rust, he returns it to us all-clean and shining. So too, God takes this nature of ours when it is rusted with the rust of sin, when our faults have covered it with abundant soot, and when it has destroyed the beauty he put into it in the beginning, and he smelts it anew. He plunges it into the waters as into the smelting furnace and lets the grace of the Spirit fall on it instead of the flames. He then brings us forth from the furnace, renewed like newly moulded vessels, to rival the rays of the sun with brightness. He has broken the old man to pieces, but has produced a new man who shines brighter than the old.

John Chrysostom

The water of baptism is a furnace

It behoves you to think that you are going into the water as into a furnace, where you will be renewed and refashioned in order that you may move to a higher nature, after having cast away your old mortality and fully assumed an immortal and incorruptible nature. These things dealing with birth happen to you in the water, because you were fashioned at the beginning from earth and water.

Theodore

THE IDENTIFICATION MARK OF CHRIST

First you receive a sign on your forehead. This is the highest and noblest part of the body; when we are talking to somebody, it is to this part that we direct our eyes. So you receive this mark on the forehead to show what a great privilege you are receiving. 'For now we see in a mirror dimly, but then face to face.' We all, with unveiled face, beholding the glory of the Lord, are being changed into his likeness from one degree of glory to another. This is why we have to receive the seal on the upper part of the face. In this way the demons can see it a long way off and are deterred from coming close to harm us in future; and we proclaim that God has granted us the privilege of beholding henceforth with face unveiled, if only we display before him the sign that we are members of his household and soldiers of Christ our Lord . . .

Now that you carry the identification-mark of a soldier of Christ our Lord, you may receive the rest of the sacraments and so acquire the full armour of the Spirit and your share in the heavenly blessings.

Theodore

'I believe'

Since God is invisible by nature, to face him and promise to persevere as members of his household you need faith. The blessings that
God is preparing for us in heaven by the administration of Christ
our Lord, the blessings that we hope for when we present ourselves
for baptism – these are invisible and indescribable too. For this
reason too we must have faith in these invisible blessings in store for
us . . . That is why the words 'I believe', are followed by the words 'I
am baptised'. For it is in faith that you come forward to receive the
holy gift of baptism; you mean to be reborn, to die with Christ and
rise again with him, in order that this second birth may replace your
first and obtain for you a share in heaven . . .

To the foregoing words you add: 'In the name of the Father and
of the Son and of the Holy Spirit'. For such is God's nature. It is the
Substance which existed from all eternity, the cause of all, which
created us in the beginning and now it is renewing us; it is Father,
Son and Holy Spirit.

Theodore

The white garment

Now that you have put off your old garments and put on those
which are spiritually white, you must go clad in white all your days.
I do not, of course, mean that your ordinary clothes must always be
white, but that you must be clad in those true, spiritual garments
which are white and shining. Then you will be able to say with the
blessed Isaiah: 'Let my soul rejoice in the Lord; for he has dressed
me in the garments of salvation, and with the robe of gladness he
has clothed me'.

Cyril

THE LIVING WATER OF THE HOLY SPIRIT

'The water that I shall give him will become in him a spring of water welling up to eternal life.' This is a new kind of water, living, welling up, welling up for those who are worthy. Why did he call the grace of the Spirit water? Because all things depend on water. Water produces herbs and living things. Water comes down from heaven as rain: water always comes down in the same form yet its effects are manifold – thus it takes one form in the palm-tree and another in the vine; it is in all things and takes all forms, though it is uniform and always remains itself. For the rain does not change, coming down now as one thing and now as another but it adapts itself to the nature of the things which receive it and it becomes what is appropriate to each.

Cyril

The fruits of baptism

The power of holy baptism consists in this: it implants in you the hope of future benefits, enables you to participate in the things which we expect, and by means of the symbols and signs of the future good things it informs you with the gift of the Holy Spirit, the first fruits of whom you receive when you are baptised.

The working of the Holy Spirit is that it is in the hope of the future things that you receive the grace of baptism, and that you draw nigh unto the gift of baptism in order to die and to rise with Christ so that you may be born again to the new life, and thus, after having been led by these symbols to the participation in the realities, you will perform the symbol of that true second birth.

Theodore

AN ADVANCE PAYMENT

Baptism assures us of the resurrection, a resurrection which in signs and symbols we already enjoy sacramentally by faith. The fact that we receive a double birth, and pass from the first to the second, need not surprise us, because even in our physical existence we receive a double birth, first from a man and then from a woman. First we are born from a man in the form of a sperm. Everyone knows that the seed bears no resemblance to a human being until it has been conceived, shaped and brought to birth by a woman according to the laws of nature decreed by God. So too at baptism we are born in seed, but not yet in the immortal nature we hope to attain at the resurrection: we do not yet bear the least resemblance to it. But if in faith and hope of the future blessings we shape ourselves by a Christian life, when the time of the resurrection comes, according to God's decree we shall receive a second birth from the dust and assume this immortal and incorruptible nature. 'Christ our Saviour', says St Paul, 'will change our lowly body to be like his glorious body'.

For the present we are born in anticipation at baptism in the hope of this expected birth. For at the moment we receive the first fruits of the grace of the Holy Spirit, which we shall possess then; today we are given an advance payment of what we shall receive in full through the resurrection in the world to come, and which will make us immortal and unchanging.

Theodore

The ongoing commitment

Keep strong and unshaken your contract with the Master, which you wrote not with ink nor on paper, but with faith and in confession. Be zealous to remain all the days of your life in the same brilliance. If we shall be willing constantly to contribute our fair share, it is possible not only to remain in this shining brightness, but even to make this spiritual robe of ours more brilliant, since Paul too, after the grace of baptism, appeared all the more bright and shining, as the grace within him bloomed forth with each passing day.

John Chrysostom

Membership of the Church

God made all men as one body of Christ at the second birth from the holy baptism, and prepared them to hope that they will participate with him in the future good things of the next world. Paul calls this Church the body of Christ because it received communion with him through the regeneration of baptism, symbolically in this world but truly and effectively in the next ...

The catechumen shows by his words: I am not preparing for baptism for the sake of little things but for the sake of great and wonderful things and heavenly benefits, as I am expecting that through baptism I shall be made a member of the Church, which is the congregation of the faithful, who through baptism become worthy to be called the body of Christ our Lord and receive an ineffable holiness and the hope of the future immortality and immutability.

Theodore

The Triduum: reflections on the crucifixion, the descent into the underworld, and the resurrection

THE LIFE-GIVING CROSS

How precious is the gift of the cross!
See, how beautiful it is to behold!
It shows no sign of evil mixed with good, like the tree of old in
    Eden;
it is all beautiful and comely to see and to taste.

For it is a tree which brings forth life, not death.
It is the source of light, not darkness.
It offers you a home in Eden.
It does not cast you out.
It is the tree which Christ mounted as a king his chariot,
and so destroyed the devil, the lord of death,
and rescued the human race from slavery to the tyrant.

It is the tree on which the Lord,
like a great warrior with his hands and feet and his divine side
    pierced in battle,
healed the wounds of our sins,
healed our nature that had been wounded by the evil serpent.

Of old we were poisoned by a tree;
now we have found immortality through a tree.
Of old we were led astray by a tree;
now we have repelled the treacherous snake by means of a tree.
Indeed what an unheard-of exchange!
We are given life instead of death.

   Theodore the Studite (759–826)

The cross and the underworld

Our Lord was trodden underfoot by death, and in turn trod upon death as upon a road . . . For our Lord went out carrying his cross, according to death's wish; he cried out on the cross and led the dead out from hell, against death's wish. He entered death's domain, broke open its strong-room and scattered the treasure.

This glorious son of the carpenter, who set up his cross above the all-consuming world of the dead, led the human race into the abode of life. Because through the tree the human race had fallen into the regions below, he crossed over on the tree of the cross into the abode of life . . .

Glory to you! You built your cross as a bridge over death, so that departed souls might pass from the realm of death to the realm of life.

You are alive! Your murderers handled your life like farmers: they sowed it like grain deep in the earth, for it to spring up and raise with itself a multitude of men.

Come, let us offer him the great, universal sacrifice of our love, and pour out before him our richest hymns and prayers. For he offered his cross to God as a sacrifice in order to make us all rich.

Ephrem the Syrian (c. 306–73)

HOLY SATURDAY: THE DESCENT INTO HELL

What is happening?
Today there is a great silence over the earth,
a great silence, and stillness,
a great silence because the King sleeps;
the earth was in terror and was still,
because God slept in the flesh and raised up those
who were sleeping from the ages.

God has died in the flesh, and the underworld has trembled.
Truly he goes to seek out our first parent like a lost sheep;
he wishes to visit those who sit in darkness and in the shadow of
    death.
He goes to free the prisoner Adam and his fellow-prisoner Eve
    from their pains,
he who is God and Adam's son.
The Lord goes into them holding his victorious weapon, his cross.
When Adam, the first created man, sees him,
he strikes his breast in terror and calls out to all:
'My Lord be with you all'.
And Christ in reply says to Adam:
'And with your spirit'.
And grasping his hand he raises him up, saying
'Awake, O sleeper,
and arise from the dead,
and Christ shall give you light.'

'I am your God, who for your sake became your son,
who for you and your descendants now speak
and command with authority those in prison:
Come forth,
and those in darkness:
Have light,
and those who sleep:

Rise . . .

> 'I command you:
> Awake, sleeper,
> I have not made you to be held a prisoner in the
> underworld.
> Arise from the dead; I am the life of the dead.
> Arise, O man, work of my hands,
> arise, you who were fashioned in my image.
> Rise, let us go hence;
> for you in me and I in you,
> together we are one undivided person.'

A reading from an ancient homily for Holy Saturday

EASTER: THE LIGHT OF CHRIST

Christ's resurrection is life for the dead, pardon for sinners, glory for the saints. And so the holy prophet invites every creature to the celebration of Christ's resurrection: we should rejoice, he says, and be glad on this day which the Lord has made.

The light of Christ is day without night, day without end. Understanding that day to be Christ, Saint Paul says: 'The night is far gone, the day is at hand'. 'The night is far gone', he says, it is not approaching; for he wishes you to understand that when Christ's light draws near, the darkness of the devil is put to flight, and the shadows of sin do not approach; the old gloom is dispelled by the endless brightness, and the insidious approach of wrongdoing is halted.

Christ is the Son-day, to whom the Father-day has whispered the secret of his divinity. He is the day who says through the mouth of Solomon: 'I have made an undying light rise in the heavens'.

And so, my brethren, we ought all to rejoice on this holy day. No one should separate himself from the general rejoicing because he has sins on his conscience; no one should refuse to take part in the public worship because of the burden of his misdeeds. However great a sinner he may be, on this day he should not despair of pardon, for the privileges granted by this day are great. If a thief should be thought worthy of paradise, why should not a Christian be thought worthy of forgiveness?

Maximus of Turin (c. 380–c. 465)

Easter: the radiant feast

Rejoice!
If any be a devout lover of God,
let him partake with gladness from this fair and radiant feast.
If any be a faithful servant,
let him enter rejoicing into the joy of his Lord.

Enter then, all of you, into the joy of our Lord,
first and last, receive alike your reward . . .
Rich and poor dance together.
You who have fasted and you who have not fasted, rejoice
  together.
The table is fully laden: let all enjoy it.
The calf is fatted: let none go away hungry.

Let none lament his poverty;
for the universal kingdom is revealed.
Let none bewail his transgressions;
for the light of forgiveness has risen from the tomb.
Let none fear death;
for the death of the Saviour has set us free.

Christ is risen! And you, O death, are annihilated!
Christ is risen! And the evil ones are cast down!
Christ is risen! And the angels rejoice!
Christ is risen! And life is liberated!
Christ is risen! And the tomb is emptied of its dead;
for Christ having risen from the dead,
is become the first-fruits of those who have fallen asleep.

John Chrysostom

A NEW SONG

We are told to sing to the Lord a new song.
A new man knows a new song.
A song is a thing of joy,
and if we think carefully about it,
a thing of love.
So the man who has learned to love a new life
has learned to sing a new song.

My brothers, my sons, children of the catholic church, holy seeds
    of heaven,
you who have been born again in Christ,
born from above,
Listen to me, or rather, through me
'Sing to the Lord a new song'.
'But I do sing' you may reply.
You sing, of course you sing, I can hear you;
But make sure that your life sings the same tune as your mouth.

Sing with your voices,
Sing with your hearts,
Sing with your lips,
Sing with your lives.

'Sing to the Lord a new song.'
Do you ask what you should sing about the one whom you love?
Of course you want to sing about the one you love.
Do you ask what you should sing in praise of him?
Listen:
'His praise is in the assembly of the saints'.
The singer himself is the praise contained in the song.

Do you want to speak the praise of God?
Be yourselves what you speak.
If you live good lives,
you are his praise.

Augustine of Hippo (354–430)

Notes

1. This phrase is taken from an article, 'A time to be born', by James Leachman OSB, a monk of Ealing Abbey, written in the *Tablet*, 15 March 2008, p. 19. There has been much interesting material on Easter and the paschal mysteries in recent years. I found particularly illuminating 'Caught between earth and heaven', by Daniel O'Leary, a priest of the Leeds diocese living in West Yorkshire, *Tablet*, 15 April 2006, p. 11; 'Vigil of fire and water', by Fr Martin Jakubas, a parish priest in Sussex, *Tablet*, 15 April 2006, p. 29; and 'Lighten the darkness', by Paul Bailey, a Rite of Christian Initiation Adviser, *Tablet*, 7 April 2007, p. 27. These all bring their different perspectives and write out of their own experiences of recent practice.

2. It is good to remember that entry into the monastery or convent was often seen as a second baptism, a deepening and strengthening of the original experience of baptism. See Demetrius Dumm OSB, *Christ Above All: The Bible in the Rule of Benedict*, Leominster, Gracewing, 1996, p. 24.

3. For the full text, see *The Divine Office*, The Liturgy of the Hours according to the Roman Rite, 3 vols, London, Collins, 1974 (reprinted 1998), vol. I, pp. 330–2. This is a source to which I shall make frequent reference (it will appear in future as *Divine Office*) since it makes the writings of the early Fathers easily accessible in the office of readings, which offers extracts throughout the liturgical year.

4. This comes from his homily on the Gospel of John, and is chosen for his day, 10 November, *Divine Office*, vol. III, p. 387.

5. *Saint Benedict's Rule,* translation and introduction by Patrick Barry OSB, former abbot of Ampleforth, Mahwah NJ, Hidden Spring, 2004. See particularly the section on *lectio divina* in the Introduction, pp. 12–16.

6. Bonnie Thurston, 'Holy Saturday', in *Hints and Glimpses*, Abergavenny, Three Peaks Press, 2004, p. 47.

7. See *Divine Office*, vol. II, pp. 320–2, where this superb piece of writing can be read in its entirety.

8. Karl Rahner SJ, *The Eternal Year*, London, 1964, p. 90.

9. Ibid., p. 91.

10. See Malcolm Thurlby, *The Herefordshire School of Romanesque Sculpture*, Herefordshire, Logaston Press, 1999. (The Eardisley font is shown on the dedication page to Zoe.)

11. Rowan Williams, *The Dwelling of the Light: Praying with Icons of Christ*, Norwich, Canterbury Press, 2003, pp. 31–43. See also Leonid Ouspensky and Vladimir Lossky, *The Meaning of Icons*, Crestwood NY, St Vladimir's Seminary Press, 1989, pp. 185–7.

12. Words by Friedrich von Spee (1591–1635), trans. Percy Dearmer.

13. Melito of Sardis, homily for the Pasch, which is set for the office of readings for Monday of the Easter Octave. See *Divine Office*, vol. II, pp. 367–8.

14. Éamon Ó Carragáin, *The City of Rome and the World of Bede*, Jarrow lecture, 1994. I quote this in an article on the 'Synod of Whitby', in *I Have Called You Friends: Essays on Reconciliation in Honour of Frank Griswold*, Cambridge MA, Cowley Publications, 2006, pp. 29–45.

15. Bede, *A History of the English Church and People*, V.21.

16. See Benedicta Ward SLG, *A True Easter: The Synod of Whitby 664 AD*, Fairacres Publications, Oxford, SLG Press, 2007.

17. Ruth Bidgood, *Symbols of Plenty: Selected Longer Poems*, Norwich, Canterbury Press, 2006, p. 57.

18. I cannot remember where I read this phrase but it stayed in my mind as a vivid way of describing the price we pay for this.

19. Andrew Chandler, in his introduction to *Humanitas: The Journal of the George Bell Institute*, 3.1, October 2001.

20. These are the opening words of a Latin text attributed to St Basil of Caesaria: 'The *Admonitio ad filium spiritualem*', Introduction and trans. Robert Rivers OSB and Harry Hagan OSB, *American Benedictine Review*, 53.1, March 2002, pp. 121–46.

21. Rule 73.5. This is discussed in two useful articles: Michael Casey OCSO, 'Ascetic and ecclesial reflections on RB 73.5', *Tjurunga* 28, 1985; and Thomas Keating OSB, 'The two streams of coenobitic tradition in the Rule of St Benedict', *Cistercian Studies*, XI.4, 1976, pp. 257–68.

22. Society of St John the Evangelist, *Living in Hope: A Rule of Life for Today*, introduced by Martin L. Smith SSJE, Cambridge MA, Cowley Publications, 1997, and Norwich, Canterbury Press, 2000.

23. Thomas Merton, *School of Charity*, ed. Patrick Hart, New York, Farrar, Strauss & Giroux, 1990.

24. Francis Kline, *Lovers of the Place: Monasticism Loose in the Church*, Collegeville MN, Liturgical Press, 1997. The first quotation comes from p. 29, the rest are taken from the Introduction.

25. That phrase is taken from Eckhart Tolle, *The Power of Now: A Guide to Spiritual Enlightenment*, New World Library, 1999; London, Hodder & Stoughton, 2001.

26. This most fascinating topic is explored in Paul F. Bradshaw and Lawrence Hoffman (eds), *Passover and Easter: The Symbolic Structuring of Sacred Seasons*, Indiana, University of Notre Dame Press, 1991.

27. 'Easter – the awkward time of the year', *Daily Telegraph*, 26 March 2005.

28. *Divine Office*, vol. II, p. 246.

29. *Carmina Gadelica*, ed. Angus Mathieson, Edinburgh, Scottish Academic Press, 1954, vol. 5. This volume is less well known since it is not specifically religious, but contains folklore material.

30. A. M. Allchin and Esther de Waal (eds), *Threshold of Light: Prayers and Praises from the Celtic Tradition*, London, Darton, Longman & Todd, 2004 [1986], p. x. Published in the USA as *Prayers and Praises in the Celtic Tradition*, Illinois, Templegate.

31. *Saint Benedict's Rule*, translation and introduction by Patrick Barry OSB, pp. 1, 8–9.

32. Anne Field OSB, *From Darkness to Light: How One Became a Christian in the Early Church*, Ben Lomond CA, Conciliar Press, 1997, p. 49. (Originally published in England as *New Life*, Oxford, A. R. Mowbray & Co., 1980.)

33. Mircea Eliade, *Images and Symbols: Studies in Religious Symbolism*, Princeton University Press, 1991, p. 16.

34. Quoted in the Introduction to *Selected Poems of Thomas Merton*, New Directions, 1967, p. xiii. The letter was dated 1954.

35. Charles Jencks, *Towards a Symbolic Architecture*, London, Rizzoli, 1985, p. 22.

36. See the *Proceedings of the American Benedictine Academy Convention*, August 1994, ed. Renée Branigan OSB, Mott ND, Eido Printing. Also of interest are the *Pre-Convention Reflection Papers*, October 1993, Yankton SD, Sacred Heart Monastery. I was fortunate enough to be present at Atchison, Kansas, for the Convention.

37. Terrence Kardong OSB, 'Symbol and Ritual in the Rule of St Benedict: An Exploration', in *Proceedings*, pp. 95–105.

38. Bonnie Thurston, 'Words and the Word', *The Way*, 44.2, April 2005, p. 16.

39. Flannery O'Connor, *The Habit of Being: Letters of Flannery O'Connor*, ed. Sally Fitzgerald, New York, Vintage Books, 1980, p. 70.

40. The ideas here owe much to a sermon by Dean Sam Lloyd preached in Washington National Cathedral, February 2005.

41. I owe this quotation to Michael Whelan SM, the Director of the Aquinas Academy in Sydney, Australia, in a paper presented to the Melbourne Catholic Education Conference, 3 June 2002.

42. Luci Shaw, 'Art and Christian spirituality: companions in the Way', *Direction*, 27.2, Fall 1998.

43. This is not the place to write about number symbolism, or the significance of plants, the physical elements and their different levels of meaning, or how the signs of the zodiac were as familiar in cathedrals as in small local churches. The list could go on and on, and the enthusiasm for Celtic spirituality may well be a reflection of a hunger for a world that has levels of awareness lying below the surface.

44. Sebastian Brock, *Luminous Eye: The Spiritual World Vision of St Ephrem*, Kalamazoo, Cistercian Publications, 1992.

45. Christopher Calderhead, *Illuminating the Word: The Making of the Saint John's Bible*, Collegeville MN, Liturgical Press, 2006, p. 21. There are to be seven volumes in full colour but reproductions of each page will be separately available for purchase.

. I am fortunate enough to have a double connection with this great enterprise. I live only a few miles from the Scriptorium where Donald Jackson and his team are working, and I have been able to see the work in progress. But I also have a very special link with the community who some years ago did me the great honour of giving me an honorary doctorate for my work in the field of monastic and ecumenical studies.

46. 'New Words for God: contemplation and religious writing', in Paul M. Pearson, Danny Sullivan and Ian Thomson (eds), *Thomas Merton: Poet, Monk, Prophet*, papers given at the Thomas Merton Society Conference March 1996, Abergavenny, Three Peaks Press, pp. 39–48.

47. Thomas Merton, *Contemplation in a World of Action*, Image Books, 1973, p. 357.

48. See the new edition, Thomas Merton, *Seeking Paradise: The Spirit of the Shakers*, ed. Paul Pearson, Maryknoll NY, Orbis Books, 2003.

49. See her paper in the *American Benedictine Academy Pre-Convention Reflection Papers*, 'Suggested sources for a study of symbolism: creating a renewed monastic environment, symbol, ritual and practice', op. cit., pp. 15–20.

50. Martin Smith, *Compass and Stars*, New York, Seabury Press, 2007, p. 51.

51. Thomas M. Finn, *Baptism and the Catechumenate*, Collegeville MN, Liturgical Press, 1992, p. 1.

52. Quoted in Raymond Burnish, *The Meaning of Baptism*, London, SPCK, 1983, p. 3, n20.

53. This comes from Philoxenus and I owe it to Kilian McDonnell OSB, *The Baptism of Jesus in the Jordan: The Trinitarian and Cosmic Order of Salvation*, Collegeville MN, Liturgical Press, 1996, p. 756.

54. I owe this quotation to Edward Yarnold, *The Awe-Inspiring Rites of Initiation*, Edinburgh, T & T Clark, 1971, pp. 8–9. The original account is to be found in *Egeria's Travels*, ed. John Wilkinson, London, SPCK, 1971, whose translation gives much fascinating and valuable information, revised Jerusalem, 1981.

55. Yarnold, op. cit., p. 7.

56. Burnish, op. cit., p. 57.

57. H. M. Riley, *Christian Initiation*, Studies in Christian Antiquity 17, Washington DC, The Catholic University of America Press, 1974, p. 74.

58. Cyril of Jerusalem, quoted in Yarnold, op. cit., pp. 70–4.

59. John Chrysostom, quoted in Burnish, op. cit., p. 39.

60. Theodore of Mopsuestia, quoted by Burnish, op. cit., p. 57.

61. Theodor Klaus, *A Short History of the Western Liturgy*, trans. John Halliburton, Oxford University Press, 1969, p. 85.

62. This is from John Chrysostom, taken from two slightly different translations to be found in Burnish, op. cit., pp. 43–4, and Halliburton, op. cit., p. 79.

63. Burnish, op. cit., pp. 13–14.

64. Cyril of Jerusalem, from a catechetical lecture.

65. From a paschal homily of an ancient author.

66. I have taken this from a lecture delivered in August 1977 at the Theological Institute, Holy Cross Abbey, Colorado, reprinted in *Liturgy*. For the fuller study see Aidan Kavanagh OSB, *The Shape of Baptism: The Rite of Christian Initiation*, New York, Pueblo Press, 1978.

67. Instruction to the newly baptized at Jerusalem, which I have taken from the reading set for Thursday in the Easter Octave, *Divine Office*, vol. II, pp. 404–5.

68. Burnish, op. cit., p. 67.

69. Ibid., p. 47.

70. See Yarnold, op. cit., p. 33.

71. My earlier book, *A Life-Giving Way: A Commentary on the Rule of St Benedict*, was intended to encourage a prayerful and contemplative approach. It is published in England by Continuum and in America by the Liturgical Press.

72. See Dumm, *Christ Above All*.

73. This is why the edition of the Rule by George Holzherr OSB, abbot of Einsiedeln, is so valuable: *The Rule of Benedict: A Guide to Christian Living*, Dublin, Four Courts Press, 1994. Everything in the text that can be associated with any scriptural source appears in capital letters and there are references in the margins. It was originally written in 1982, but translated by the monks of Glenstal Abbey in 1994 and re-issued in Ireland, published by the Four Courts Press.

74. In his column in the *Tablet*, 2 April 2005.

75. *Saint Benedict's Rule*, translation and introduction by Patrick Barry OSB, p. 14.

76. Terrence Kardong OSB, *Benedict's Rule: A Translation and Commentary*, Collegeville MN, Liturgical Press, 1996, p. 28.

77. Ibid., p. 13.

78. This is taken from the Preface to his translation of the Rule which is intended for the use of lay people. *Saint Benedict's Rule*, translation and introduction by Patrick Barry OSB.

79. I have taken this from a letter written to the oblates of St Benedict's convent, St Joseph, Minnesota, by Sr Mary Anthony Wagner OSB and I have included it as an act of homage and gratitude to someone whose teachings have helped and influenced so many people.

80. Sr Laurentia Johns OSB, 'How our hearts burned within us', *Tablet*, 10 May 2008, pp. 8–9.

81. A great deal has been written on this subject. Here are a few suggestions for further reading. Michael Casey OCSO, *The Art of the Sacred Reading*, Melbourne, Dove, 1995; Michael Casey OCSO, *Sacred Reading*, Ligouri, Triumph Books, 1996; Martin L. Smith SSJE, *The Word is Very Near You: A Guide to Praying with Scripture,* Cambridge MA, Cowley Publications, 1989; Enzo Bianchi, *Praying the Word: An Introduction to Lectio Divina*, Kalamazoo MI, Cistercian Publications, 1998. There is in addition a short article by Michael Casey OCSO, 'The art of *lectio divina*', *The Benedictine Handbook*, Norwich, Canterbury Press, 2003, pp. 106–10.

82. *Saint Benedict's Rule*, translation and introduction by Patrick Barry OSB, p. 37.

83. The reference to Tom Gunn comes in a letter to Sylvia Plath, dated

1 and 2 October 1956, *Letters of Ted Hughes*, ed. Christopher Reid, London, Faber & Faber, 2007.

84. 'Listen . . . Listen again' is in fact a quotation from the opening lines of St Ambrose in instructing the candidates for baptism.

85. The phrase 'trumpet call' comes from Damasus Winzen OSB, from a conference that he gave in 1960 at Mount Saviour Monastery, near Elmira, in upstate New York, the monastery which he founded in 1951, after he fled Germany to escape Nazi persecution. It was transcribed and edited for publication in 1975–6 as *Conferences on the Prologue to the Rule*. He has many illuminating things to say about the Prologue and he gave me the idea of the heart as the inner secret of a person.

86. When I quote verse 19, I do so using the translation of Kardong because I feel that it brings out the warmth of Benedict's tone of voice more strongly. In general I follow the RB80, which here says, 'What, dear brothers, is more delightful than this voice of the Lord calling us?' (19).

87. 'Holding himself still before the gaze' are words taken from the Dialogues of St Gregory the Great as he tells us about the life of Benedict. There are many editions and translations available. It is a work that gives us incomparable glimpses into Benedict's life.

88. There is so much that is written about listening and the silence that I talk of in the final paragraph. Among recent books, see Bill Kirkpatrick, *The Creativity of Listening*, London, Darton, Longman & Todd, 2005. Although it may seem like self-advertisement what I have said myself in an earlier book is intended to be thoroughly practical in helping to practise the art of attentiveness: *Lost in Wonder*, London, Canterbury Press, 2003; Collegeville MN, Liturgical Press, 2003.

89. The striking phrase about Benedict looking into our eyes is taken from Patrick Barry OSB, in *Saint Benedict's Rule*, pp. 1–2. 'St Benedict never quite forgets the individual standing before him, into whose eyes he is looking as he offers sympathetic guidance to one God in the world of the sixth century. It was a world similar to ours but like our world in its mixture of conflict, decay, new vision, and baffling confusion.'

90. The interpretation of 'son' as prodigal is something I owe to Damasus Winzen OSB.

91. Henri Nouwen, *The Return of the Prodigal Son: A Meditation on Fathers, Brothers and Sons*, was originally published in New York by Doubleday in 1992, and has since then gone through many editions. It remains for me one of his best books (together with *The Genesee Diary*), a classic text to which one can return many times.

92. From Cyril of Jerusalem.

93. Patrick Barry OSB, in *Saint Benedict's Rule*, p. 23.

94. Frank T. Griswold, *Going Home: An Invitation to Jubilee*, Cambridge MA, Cowley Publications, 2000, pp. 1, 77. I owe much of what I say here to this small book.

95. Henri Nouwen and Philip Roderick, *Beloved: Henri Nouwen in Conversation*, Grand Rapids, Eerdmans, 2007.

96. The sentence that I wanted to rewrite is taken from Kardong's commentary on the Rule.

97. For an article on the baptismal context of Chapter 4, see Lazare de Seilhac OSB, 'The dynamism of a living stability', *Benedictines*, 47.2, 1994, p. 37.

98. What I say about the icon of the transfiguration owes much to Rowan Williams, *The Dwelling of the Light*, pp. 1–21, and to Ouspensky and Lossky, *The Meaning of Icons*, pp. 209–11. It was the commentary of Terrence Kardong OSB that first made the connection for me.

99. From an article by Mary Forman OSB, *American Benedictine Review*, September 2000.

100. Clare Amos has written a fascinating article and it is from her that I have taken the phrase 'staging-post'. 'A staging-post on the journey: transfiguration and the Anglican way', *Journal of the Anglican and Eastern Churches Association*, no. 53, Easter 2008, pp. 4–13.

101. I owe the interpretation of *deificum lumen* to Patrick Barry OSB, *Saint Benedict's Rule*, p. 15.

102. In this paragraph I have plagiarized something from Kardong's commentary, where he is commenting on the use of the Latin adverb *efficaciter* in verse 1, 'put into action': 'insistence on concrete action is typical of ancient monasticism, which was much more a lifestyle than a theory', op. cit., p. 7.

103. The three translations are those of RB80, Patrick Barry OSB and Terrence Kardong OSB respectively.

104. I owe this comment to Kardong.

105. This reading is set for Monday of the Easter Octave, in *Divine Office*, vol. II, pp. 367–8.

106. I owe this suggestive comment to Gilbert Cope, *Symbolism in the Bible and the Early Church*, London, SCM Press, 1959, p. 100.

Acknowledgements of Sources

The author and publisher are grateful for permission to reproduce copyright material from the following sources.

Texts

Biblical quotations are not attributed to any particular version, but are reproduced from the variety of sources used.

The Prologue, RB80, *The Rule of St Benedict*, in Latin and English with Notes, edited by Timothy Fry OSB, Collegeville MN, Liturgical Press, 1981.

Bonnie Thurston, 'Holy Saturday', in *Hints and Glimpses*, Abergavenny, Three Peaks Press, 2004.

Society of St John the Evangelist, *Living in Hope: A Rule for Life for Today*, introduced by Martin L. Smith SSJE, Cambridge MA, Cowley Publications, 1997; and Norwich, Canterbury Press, 2000.

Illustrations

Zoe with her mother Georgina at Eardisley font. Photo by Thomas de Waal.

Illustration from *The Four Gospels*. Decorated by Eric Gill, The Golden Cockerel Press, 1931. Houghton Rare Book Library, Washington National Cathedral.

The Baptism. Detail of twelfth-century font, Castle Frome, Herefordshire. Drawing by John Piper.

The Resurrection, Russian 15th century. Public domain image available on Wikimedia Commons at http://commons.wikimedia.org/wiki/Image: Russian_Resurrection_icon.jpg

Canterbury Cathedral crypt. Photo by Su-lin. Image available under a Creative Commons license at flickr.com/1408/1425145446_73569.

The David Jones paintings, The Royal Banners (detail), *Vexilla Regis*, 1949; The Waterfall, *Afon Honddu Fach*, 1926; and The Fountain, 1929 are used by permission of Anthony Hyne for the David Jones Estate. The author and publisher are grateful to the David Jones Society for supplying the image of The Fountain, photograph by Aled Rhys Hughes.

Heather Williams Durka, Saint Benedict icon.

Transfiguration of Christ, Sinai, 12th century. Public domain image available on Wikimedia Commons at http://commons.wikimedia.org/wiki/Image:Transfiguration_of_Christ_Icon_Sinai_12th_century.jpg

Romanesque font, *c.* 1170, St Michael's Castle Frome, Herefordshire.